M000189143

The Book On Facebook Marketing

To Help You Set Your Business & Life on Fire

Nick Unsworth

Valerie Shoopman

The Book On Facebook Marketing: To Help You Set Your Business & Life On Fire

By Nick Unsworth and Valerie Shoopman

Crescendo Publishing, LLC
300 Carlsbad Village Drive
Ste. 108A, #443
Carlsbad, California 92008-2999
Cover Design by Re Perez and Melodye Hunter

ISBN: 978-0-9960761-7-3 (p)
ISBN: 978-0-9960761-9-7 (e)

A MESSAGE FROM THE AUTHORS...

Click on the video or the link to hear a personal message from Nick + Val, authors of *The Book On Facebook Marketing: To Help You Set Your Business & Life On Fire.*

http://youtu.be/lWfuCgyTMf0

To enhance your reading experience, we've also created some rockin' videos and other downloadable goodies to help you implement all the cool strategies we've laid out in this book. You can get immediate access to everything here:

http://www.thebookonfbmarketing.com/resources

WE DEDICATE THIS BOOK ...

From Nick...

I dedicate this book to my father, "Pops."

I really can't thank you enough for all the time you spent helping me edit this very book. You're "word-smith-ery" is much appreciated.

Most importantly, I want to thank you for instilling me with integrity, an incredibly high standard, and a work ethic that will never quit.

You're the hardest working man I've ever met and I now realize that work ethic is my secret weapon as an entrepreneur. Well that, and Facebook marketing of course!

Love you!

Nick

From Valerie...

First, I'd like to thank Nick Unsworth for always dreaming big and then seeing how he can include others in his big dreams. Nick is a true inspiration, always giving me the confidence that I can do bigger and better things than what I had thought was possible. He not only inspires me, but then also helps lay the path to make it happen.

Next, I'd like to thank my family; my husband Keith and my two sons Corey and Bret. They've lived with me saying "no", "not right now", or "later" a lot more than usual with no blowback and no hard feelings. They have been there to support me through the good times and the tough times and for that I'm eternally grateful.

In gratitude to you all,

Valerie

TABLE OF CONTENTS

PART 1

PART 2

PART 1

The Book on Facebook Marketing

1. Overview and How to Maximize this Book
2. Nick's Journey: Discovering Facebook Marketing the Hard Way
3. The Power of Earned Media and Contests
4. How to Attract Ideal Customers with a Lead Magnet and Facebook Marketing Funnel
5. Narrow Your Niche, Grow Rich, and Have a Purpose-Driven Business
6. How to Write Your Own Checks with a Webinar Marketing Funnel

Nick Unsworth and Valerie Shoopman

Chapter 1

Overview and How to Maximize this Book

-1-

Overview and How to Maximize this Book

Hey hey! So first and foremost, I would like to congratulate you on your purchase of *The Book on Facebook Marketing*. It's a book that can completely change your trajectory by providing you with that one tiny, missing piece that unlocks your inner greatness and gets you and your business to the next level.

Ask me, "How do you know?"

My mother (a.k.a. Mama Celeste Unsworth) gave me a book in 2008 that completely changed my mindset. That mindset shift then changed how I think, which changed what showed up in my life, which then changed my business and life forever. The book was *The Secret*, and I highly encourage you to read it as a companion to this book.

I've found that the most successful entrepreneurs invest in themselves with both their time and money. Reading books to get ahead and hiring mentors and coaches are some of the fastest ways to get where you want to go with far less pain along the way.

It's the difference between running your first Facebook ad and losing your shirt versus getting the training you need so that you can run your first Facebook ad and earn a positive return on your investment.

One thing that I've learned the hard way is that you have to be careful when it comes to taking advice. When I was twenty years old, I spent two years of my life with a mentor who turned out to be completely full of BS. The car he drove, the house he rented ... everything was a farce, a façade, a big ol' pile of BS to entice people to invest their time and their money into his business opportunity.

You can rest assured that this book is based on facts. We're going to tell you the good, the bad, and the ugly.

The nice thing is that Facebook offers a lot of benefits for your business when you know how to effectively market on that platform.

So to give you a little perspective on me, I've been marketing on Facebook for almost five years. In some industries five years isn't a lot of time, but for Facebook marketing, it means that I've been around and learning the advertising platform since its infancy.

I've coached over 1,750 entrepreneurs on how to leverage Facebook marketing and have consulted for companies like Keller Williams Real Estate, Safeco Insurance, and *New York Times* best-selling authors John Assaraf and Brian Tracy.

I've spoken all over the United States and Canada and have been featured in popular Facebook marketing books and industry-leading websites.

My co-author, team member, and dear friend Valerie "The Shoop" Shoopman has a background in teaching and is literally the best in the industry at Facebook advertising. She has helped my company Life on Fire go from a start-up to a seven-figure business in less than two years by leveraging her talents with Facebook advertising.

Valerie will walk you through everything you need to know to be successful with Facebook marketing and advertising in later chapters.

Now that you've had a brief exposure to our background and credentials, let me share the benefits of Facebook marketing.

Benefits of Facebook Marketing:

- Create sales and positive cash flow in your business—everything from making your first $100 online all the way to a seven-figure revenue that is directly tracked to Facebook marketing.
- Instantly position yourself as an expert within your industry.
- Gain exposure and build your brand awareness.

- Grow your e-mail list as big as you would like via Facebook ads.
- Build a tribe of raving fans, a.k.a. "likes."

Imagine what your life would look like if you had an abundance of cash flow, leads, and "likes" on Facebook.

What if you never had to worry about money ever again?

Imagine being able to raise your prices because of the brand positioning that Facebook gave you.

What if you always had a line out the door or a waiting list for people to buy your products or services?

What if you were able to run Facebook ads and go from six figures to seven figures in annual revenue in less than six months?

All of this is possible with Facebook marketing when you use our strategies.

How This Book is Written:

These chapters will guide you like a duck chasing breadcrumbs, and by the end of it, you'll not only be satisfied, you'll have everything you need to crush it with Facebook marketing. By "crush it" I mean create additional profit in your business so that you can live a Life on Fire.

In the first six chapters you'll hear about my journey filled with trials and tribulations. You'll also hear how I ultimately discovered exactly how to leverage Facebook marketing to achieve massive business success.

Starting in Chapter 7, Valerie Shoopman will take over to dive deeper into the "how-to" steps of mastering your Facebook marketing to create profits in your business.

How to Maximize This Book:

Step 1:

I encourage you to take a second to make the decision to commit to reading the entire book. These strategies dramatically changed my life, Valerie's life, and the lives of entrepreneurs all over the world.

Step 2:

Take advantage of our video tutorials that will guide you through the exact step-by-step process on how to set up and optimize Facebook advertising.

Go to http://www.thebookonfbmarketing.com/resources to get instant access to the tutorials.

This book will give you the strategy, and our videos will be incredibly valuable help when it comes time for you to implement them.

Step 3:

Take massive "imperfect" action. It is critically important to implement what you're learning. I once had a mentor say that the "speed of implementation" is directly related to success.

Read the entire book, roll up your sleeves, and start leveraging what you've learned to set your business and Life on Fire!

Enjoy!

Chapter 2

Nick's Journey: Discovering Facebook Marketing the Hard Way

Nick Unsworth and Valerie Shoopman

-2-

Nick's Journey: Discovering Facebook Marketing the Hard Way

Do you know what it feels like to achieve a major accomplishment in life? You know ... maybe you got an A on a term paper, just graduated college, got married, or received a big award.

Well, I was brimming with excitement as my new business—The NU Perks Card—was taking off in 2008. It took off so fast that almost immediately after launch, I found myself standing next to the mayor of my town cutting a ribbon, and my face was in all the local papers and even on TV.

A big reason this business was growing so fast was that it was all based around a story. I share my story with you in this book because I want you to truly understand the power of storytelling in your Facebook marketing

Prior to the NU Perks Card, I had been on a really bad "fail" streak in business for a couple years, which is what made the success feel so good with the NU Perks Card. People in my life that had counted me out were starting to say, "Wow, I think Unsworth is actually going to make it."

The NU Perks Card was created out of passion and purpose, which is why I think it worked so well initially.

What is the NU Perks Card?

The NU Perks Card was a physical card in the shape of a business card that folded together like an accordion. The concept was that local businesses would put discounts on the card, and I would sell the cards to consumers so that they could save money while shopping and dining out. The kicker was that 50 percent of all revenue went to charity.

So I had pounded the pavement and gone from business to business to business to ultimately get forty-five local businesses to put discounts on the card.

Oh! and by "pounded the pavement" I mean I worked my tail off. I worked like somebody was chasing me. I literally got thrown out of restaurants for waiting to speak to a manager that didn't want to speak to me. (When I say "thrown out," I mean two bouncers picked me up under the armpits and carried me out.)

It was unbelievable. I felt like I was climbing Mount Everest without a Sherpa to guide me. The biggest objection I heard was that it sounded too good to be true. "So, Nick, you're telling me that all I have to do is put a discount on this card, and you're going to do all the marketing to get more people into my store?"

Me: "Yes, sir."

Then I would face incredible resistance. It was almost as bad as if I were trying to convince them to change their religious beliefs. It was just crazy!

I share this because as entrepreneurs we are all going to face huge challenges. These challenges can take you out of the game and steal your dreams away, or you can leverage them to create an adrenaline rush of true grit to rise above and succeed.

So whether you're up against a wall in your business, or if Facebook is disapproving every ad you create, you've got to think like a winner and find a solution. There's always a way.

Finally, after a brutally challenging sales tour around my town to innumerable businesses, I got it done. I felt like I ran through the American Gladiators gauntlet about ninety times with a jousting bruise on my face, BUT I got it done and that tiny piece of progress started to gain me momentum.

I had secured some incredible discounts, such as:

- Half off the price of a bottle of wine at one of West Hartford's nicest restaurants
- Buy one appetizer and get a second appetizer free
- Get a free desert
- 15% off dry cleaning
- 20% off jewelry

Consumers could purchase the NU Perks Card for $20 and then save hundreds of dollars throughout the year by presenting the NU Perks Card where they were shopping.

My brainstorm and the key to success was that when they purchased the card for $20, there was a dropdown menu that asked where they wanted their $10 charitable donation to go. They could select from a menu of some of the most recognizable local nonprofits that I had landed to receive the money that I worked so hard to fundraise.

It was a perfect trifecta of wins.

Win – for local consumers because they could get deep discounts by marching into any business in West Hartford, Connecticut, that displayed the diamond-shaped seal of approval that stated: "We Proudly Support the NU Perks Card of West Hartford."

Win – for local businesses because this crazy entrepreneur Nick Unsworth was going to get it in the hands of everyone in town, and this would increase their foot traffic.

Win – for local charities that would receive monetary donations without having to do anything.

So ... what was in it for me?

I'm glad you asked because that's exactly what everyone asks.

"What's in it for me?" asked the consumers. They bought the NU Perks Card and reaped the perks.

"What's in it for me?" asked the business owner. They got to be on the NU Perks Card to advertise and increase traffic and sales.

"What's in it for me?" asked the nonprofits. They got the money with zero effort.

WIIFM is something I want you to highlight, circle, underline, and retain as a mental picture. Yep, it's that important.

Later in this book I'll teach you how you can take these five teeny words and leverage them to figure out EXACTLY what's going on in your prospects' minds.

The gold in marketing lies in the answer to WIIFM.

So what was in it for Nick Unsworth on the NU Perks Card?

The benefit to me was to feel dang proud each day knowing that I was slowly, silently, infecting every person that bought the card with self-gratification by doing good.

I also had the benefit of growing my brand in my local market. At the time I was also a REALTOR, and I knew that if I built up my authority and presence, I would be able to sell many more homes.

Here's a problem I encountered: People would be purchasing the card because they wanted to save money and then ... bam! The dropdown menu.

Three things would happen when they saw the dropdown menu:

1. Confusion – At first, they were confused and sometimes angry. "A $10 donation? I'm not paying an EXTRA $10 for this card!"
2. Realization – "Oh! It's part of my $20, and then I choose where my donation goes. ... I get it. Oh, wow! That's actually really cool. And dang ... I get to even choose the nonprofit that's meaningful to me!? I'm starting to like this thing a lot!"
3. Moment of higher consciousness – Upon realizing the good intent in the dropdown menu, there would come the nanosecond when the consumer would think about someone they knew that had an awful disease or disorder and then think about the positive impact of their $10.

From then on, this good feeling that the card imbued in the consumer had a lasting and multiplying effect. People began sharing it with friends, the word started to get out and spread, and sales began to dramatically increase.

This leads me into one of the most important concepts in Facebook marketing ... earned media.

You see, earned media is simply media that you earn. OK, someone once told me that I shouldn't use the same words in the definition, so let me define it this way: earned media is word of mouth. It's people telling people. The best part of earned media? You don't have to pay for it. That's why it's earned.

Are you wondering why "traditional" advertising doesn't work anymore? One of the gazillion reasons is that we live in a world where nobody trusts anyone anymore.

We just don't trust it. BUT, guess who we do trust? The Geico Lizard!! Nope. Flo the Progressive lady. Wrong again. The fifth razor on Gillette's new Mach 5? Sorry.

We trust friends.

We trust family members.

We trust people that we love and love us.

I'll dive into specific strategies as you move along in this book. (Yep, you're going to have to read the whole dang thing! Sorry, but to be super successful you can't take shortcuts. You have to become one of the 10 percent of people that purchase the book who actually make it to the end.)

OK, so, Nick, weren't we talking about your NU Perks Card? What happened!??

Really glad you asked!

So there I was, basking in the glory of good old-fashioned word-of-mouth marketing that some expert recently named "earned media." Being the optimist that I am, I decided to print 10,000 cards. (The town of West Hartford had at the time a population of about 65,000 people.) Yes ... someone once said go big or go home, and I guess I really took it to heart because at the time I thought one out of six people would be walking around town with my NU Perks Card in their hand (including children).

I may not have gotten it to one in six people, but I ended up in all the local papers and on TV on a local show called *Better Connecticut*. Seeing myself on that TV segment is one of the most embarrassing things to watch. (I had a major fear of public speaking that stemmed from high school.) Even though my performance on TV was embarrassing, I'm proud that I stepped outside my comfort zone to do it.

All growth occurs outside our comfort zone.

Anyway, people were using the cards, business owners were happy, money was being raised, and it was growing.

That's when I got a phone call that would completely change the course of my life forever. Isn't it funny to look back and realize that something as simple as a phone call would actually change your entire life direction?

My phone rang. It was an unknown number, so I timidly answered, "Hi, this is Nick Unsworth, home of the NU Perks Card of West Hartford. How can I help you today!?"

Just kidding. I answered simply, "Hi, this is Nick."

On the line was a prominent businessman in West Hartford whom I respected because everyone else seemed to. "Nick, this is Paul Stevens (not his real name) from Creeps R Us (not real name), and I've been watching what you're doing. It looks like your business is really taking off, and I have someone you should talk to."

Me: "Hey, that sounds good! Who?"

Paul Stevens: "The company is called Plummeting Profits (not real name), and they specialize in marketing and advertising. They have over 100 years of experience in the West Hartford market, and many of us local business owners use them."

Me: "Wow! Wowee! Thanks, mister!"

OK, so I was a bit of a young pup that trusted everyone. I swear I sounded cooler than that though.

Looking back, the really interesting thing to see here is that it was actually earned media (a.k.a. word of mouth) that gave me the instant sense of trust to talk to Plummeting Profits.

BUT ... since I didn't directly know Paul Stevens, the local business owner, and he wasn't on my NU Perks Card, I went out to seek further validation that Plummeting Profits was the best company in town. I spoke to about ten other local business owners, and they all said, "Yep. Plummeting Profits is the best at what they do."

I didn't ask them to define "best." I should have.

In my young entrepreneur's head I was thinking that if everyone was recommending them via earned media, then they must be good. And by "good," I thought that it would mean they would help me make profits.

"Profits" being defined as more money than I would pay them.

So ...

I headed over to good ol' Plummeting Profits and entered the boardroom. There were four advertising guys that each had twenty-five years of experience.

One guy was like Face, the character from the TV show and movie *The A-Team*. With dark black hair blown back and a nice watch, I could tell he was the main sales guy.

One guy was like Gordon Gecko, a.k.a. Michael Douglas from the movie *Wall Street*, the guy who seemed to get flushed with anger so easily it seemed like they left the majority of the client interactions to Face.

The creative guy was strikingly similar to George Costanza from *Seinfeld*, rotund in shape and with that anxious humor.

The silent guy looked like Mr. Bean. I'm not sure what he did besides give me weird looks—not funny weird looks like Mr. Bean ... mean weird looks.

So, after shaking hands aggressively, I sat down with the cast of characters.

Me: "Hey, guys, so here's my marketing plan. I want to show you how I'm bootstrapping this thing and why it's working." (Picture a ten-page Word document printed on regular white copy paper being passed from Face, to George Costanza, to Gordon Gecko, to Mr. Bean, at which point he actually started to read it until ...)

Gordon Gecko snapped his fingers, did that little "give it here" hand motion, and then literally turned on his swivel chair and tossed it in the garbage. Then he swiveled back to the table, put his elbows down, and said, "Let's talk about how to really market this business."

I was a little perplexed, but I said, "OK, Mr. Gecko, what's your advice?"

Face, Gordon, Costanza, and Mr. Bean, in unison, said: "Television commercials, radio, and print."

Me: "Oh, geez ... really? Aren't they really expensive? I didn't think they worked well."

After some back-and-forth and aggressive sales tactics, I heard a statement that I will never forget for the rest of my life.

"We have your best interest in mind."

At that point, I made the fatal mistake that costs entrepreneurs huge bucks. I didn't trust my gut.

I second-guessed myself. While I was defending my marketing plan and punching holes through theirs, they kept coming back to their experience, touting it over and over, telling me how they worked with the most prominent local businesses.

I made another mistake. I didn't have a business coach or mentor to turn to for advice.

So as I waffled on this decision, I thought to myself, "Hmm ... maybe I had a couple business failures in the past because I screwed them up. Maybe I'm the problem. Maybe I should trust these guys since others recommended them with that 'earned media' stuff. Maybe I should get out of my own way and let the professionals take the NU Perks Card to a whole new level."

So I signed my life away.

I then worked with Costanza on the TV commercial. This was a bit of a doozy because I absolutely stunk on camera.

Remember a couple pages back I mentioned my fear of speaking? Well, it apparently transferred as a fear of being on camera too. I wasn't good at it. So we went from doing a commercial that featured me to a fifteen-second animation, which was actually a pretty solid commercial.

After it was done, we talked about all the media they were purchasing on my behalf. At this point, I was already into it for about $10,000 for production costs and fees to get started with them. Then I had another $20,000 that I would be spending for media distribution over the course of two weeks.

Are you wondering how the heck a twenty-six-year-old kid could afford all this?

You remember that I said that I had failed at a couple businesses prior to the NU Perks Card? Well, I was still licking my wounds from the real estate crash in 2007. You see, I got into the industry in 2006 with just enough time to learn the industry, get my license, and work my tail off only to get completely annihilated in the market crash of 2007. So ... I didn't have a whole lot of funds to invest.

BUT a true entrepreneur will always find a way despite the challenges in front of him. Since I had already spent a ton of money to start the NU Perks Card, I was personally tapped out. So I decided to use credit cards.

After exhaustive conversations with Plummeting Profits, I was sure that this was merely for cash flow. I would have the money back within thirty days, and then I could just simply pay off the credit cards.

(Can you guess what happened next? "Plummeting Profits" is fairly obvious foreshadowing, yes?)

As I looked over the media-buying schedule, I noticed we were advertising to the entire state of Connecticut, which seemed odd. I argued that the marketing was un-targeted because my NU Perks Card worked only in West Hartford, Connecticut, but they said ...

Face, Gordon, Costanza, and Mr. Bean: "You don't understand! If you want to sell cards, you have to advertise here."

Me: "But why would we advertise to the entire state when we could just advertise on cable and advertise TV commercials just to West Hartford?"

Face, Gordon, Costanza, and Mr. Bean: "This is where we know people take action and buy. They are less targeted, but this is more effective."

The logic here didn't make sense, but again I figured that maybe I should get out of my own way and trust them. They had my best interest in mind.

So here we are ... the big moment. I triple-checked that the DVR was set to record the six o'clock news because that was where my commercial would air multiple times.

I turned off all other distractions and waited for my big moment. Just imagine if you had a commercial that aired during the Super Bowl and you put your entire life savings on it. Shoot—just imagine that you had your life savings on it PLUS a total of $30,000 in credit card debt on it.

I was literally on the edge of my seat and then bam! The NU Perks Card of West Hartford danced across the screen! Woo-hoo!! There it was, my big moment. It went by a little faster than I thought it would, but I guess that's what happens when it's only fifteen seconds long.

Then, as we were watching a bit later ... BOOM! We saw that little card dance past us again on TV! Woo-hoo!

I was picturing all the money that we would be bringing in for charity. I was fantasizing about which charity would be the most popular, wondering how many thousands would be in the merchant account. I was also picturing paying off the credit cards and some of the start-up expenses with the other half of the revenue that came in.

I whistled and skipped over to my computer and pulled up my merchant processor that showed the money that came in from NU Perks Card sales. I was totally sure that there must have been an error. It showed zero sales.

There had to have been a mistake. I just spent $10,000 on production and fees, then another straight $10,000 in advertising for seven days. I was thinking I would have made at least a couple thousand in card sales per day.

So I kept refreshing, thinking that it must be slow to report. Then I tried to call them, but they weren't open.

As soon as I woke up the next day, I ran to my computer again and refreshed the display. Still nothing. "This is so freaking weird," I thought.

I called up the merchant processor to ask them about the sales. "Nope, nothing has been processed in the last twenty-four hours, sir."

"What do you mean?" I asked. "How could that be!?"

"Umm ... well, it's pretty clear," said the merchant. "Nothing has been processed since yesterday morning."

I hung up. Nothing was making sense, so I called Plummeting Profits.

Me: "Hey Face, what's happening? Did something go wrong!? Did we not air as much as we were supposed to or something?"

Face: "Nothing is wrong. It hasn't even been a day yet. You need to relax and give the advertising time to work. We've never received a frantic call like this this early."

Me: "What do you mean, 'this early'? Do other people call you frantically like me that are in this position?"

Face: "No. And I'm not going to entertain this conversation. I'll talk to you after the results from week one are in."

So for a minute I thought maybe, just maybe there was still hope.

Days go by with no sales, and I'm totally sweating bullets. We're approaching the seventh day, which means I've burned through $10,000 with no results—no money back, no money for charity.

The day before my call with Plummeting Profits, I went to the mailbox and saw a handwritten note, which was odd. "Who still does that?" I thought.

I opened it up, and to my surprise it was an NU Perks Card sale! It was a sweet old woman out in Cheshire, Connecticut, which was about an hour drive from West Hartford. I have no idea how she found my address or why she didn't use the website, but it was a sale.

Imagine the feeling of spending $10,000 and holding a $20 check in your hand—of which half goes to charity.

My return on investment was exactly negative 990 percent.

Receiving that check was a wake-up call. I realized that there wasn't some major malfunction in the website or delivery of the ads.

I called Plummeting Profits the next day for my one-week anniversary of losing $10,000 in ad spending plus $10,000 in production costs and fees. It was World War III on the line.

I was freaking out because I had financed it all with credit cards, and they didn't seem to care about it. They kept saying the money had been spent. I needed to sit tight because it had only been a week, and we needed to keep going.

If this wasn't crazy enough, they wanted me to invest MORE money into TV commercials to increase my "frequency."

Face, Gordon, Costanza, and Mr. Bean: "Nick, we warned you. Your budget is too small. You need to invest more."

Me: "Face, are you freaking nuts? I'm into this for $20,000 after seven days, and I got one $20 card sale of which $10 goes to me and $10 goes to charity. You're seriously telling me to invest more?"

It was a disaster, and I couldn't get back my last $10,000 for the ads that were airing on week two. I had to sit back and watch another $10,000 dwindle away as the advertisement for my dream business that was designed to help others danced across the TV screen.

In week two, I sold thirteen cards for a grand total of fourteen cards sold in two weeks—off a total $30,000 budget. That's $280 in gross revenue of which $140 went to charity.

Is that what those goons were talking about when they said "frequency"?

Unbelievable!

So what went wrong?

Did my website not convert well enough?

Was it the offer?

Was it me?

Nope. It was the medium.

The TV commercials were simply NOT targeted. Why on earth would someone in a different town buy my card? Not only were the TV commercials not targeted, but they also did not appeal to a specific target market either—any person sitting in front of the TV watching the nightly news anywhere in Connecticut is not a targeted prospect.

My intended target market was moms aged twenty-seven to fifty that lived in West Hartford and were the ones making the household buying decisions and shopping in local West Hartford stores.

It did not happen as I intended, but I had to move on. I'm the kind of guy who always tries to find the positives behind adverse impacts. The silver lining. The blessings in disguise.

If you're an entrepreneur, having this attitude is absolutely imperative; otherwise, you'll get taken out after your first knockdown. You have to get good at getting up faster and faster every time your face hits the canvas after taking a big mean right hook.

So even though I was now sweating bullets about my new 30,000-pound friend I called "Jonny Debt," I couldn't let it stop me. I had to put a smile on my face and keep this dirty little secret to myself. Nobody knew—not my parents, not my girlfriend at the time, not my friends. Nobody! I kept it all in and put a smile on my face and continued with nothing more than blind faith that I would figure it out and that I would discover the hidden blessing.

That's all you can do. What's done is done. Playing the victim right there would have conceded defeat, destroyed my drive, and inevitably led to an even faster downward spiral.

So I went back to my grass-roots marketing plan using earned media or word of mouth. It fit my dire financial straits. Word of mouth sure was cost-effective. People were telling people about it, and it didn't cost me anything—quite the contrast from Plummeting Profit's approach.

So as I was doing my thing, I met with my web developer, who was freaking out because the hosting costs were coming out of his end.

"Weird Al" the web developer: "Nick, how much money are you spending on your ads? Your traffic is in the tens and tens of thousands. I haven't seen anything like it."

Me: "Well, I spent $20,000 in direct media buying."

Weird Al: "Yeah, and you told me that you ended it, right?"

Me: "Yes."

My mind was racing. Why was the traffic so high? Were the ads still showing? Was Plummeting Profits still charging me for more ads? I hoped and prayed that wasn't the case. I demanded that they stop, and they didn't have my permission to spend on my credit card. I quickly called Plummeting Profits, freaking out that they were still advertising, but they assured me that they weren't.

I told Weird Al, and we were totally perplexed. Why on earth was I getting all this traffic?

For all of you thinking, "Duh ... look at Google Analytics," keep in mind that this was in early 2008, it was my first website, and my web developer wasn't too helpful if you know what I mean. What I did learn from Google Analytics, though, was I was receiving a tremendous number of daily visitors to the site because I ranked on the first page of Google.

Then I got a package in the mail. Have you ever received one of those fancy overnight packages that you have to sign for? Well, at this point in my life, it was a rarity, and I thought it could be something exciting. So there I was, tearing open this big official package as if it was Christmas … and I pulled out this big, fat stack of papers.

As if things couldn't get worse, it was a cease-and-desist order for trademark infringement along with a threat of a huge lawsuit because my name was similar to another company's.

My heart sank. I felt the worst feeling in the world, like I was going to instantly lose everything in my life along with the sense that I was going to go to jail and would be shamed out of my community and family. I will never forget that feeling.

I was freaking out and called them up immediately.

"Excuse me, sir," they said, "we need to speak to your legal team."

Me: "Legal team? What? Dude, I'm twenty-six years old and just lost everything in this little business where all I'm trying to do is raise money for charity. Why are you doing this to me? There's nothing to take. I'm negative $30,000 on this project, and it now doesn't look like it's going to make it."

Larry the Lawyer: "Well, you see, your little company is stealing all our traffic, and it's costing us money ... lots of it."

Me: "What on earth do you mean?"

Larry the Lawyer: "On Google ... your site is outranking us and stealing our traffic."

I was thinking, "Ooh, holy moly! So THAT'S why I'm still getting all that traffic to the website?"

Me: "OK, cool. So how can I make it stop? How do I get off the first page of Google? I'm not selling many cards anyway, and it's all through word of mouth."

Larry the Lawyer: "I don't know, but if you continue to sell or use these cards, you will find yourself in court."

I ended up acting as my own lawyer, which was not a good idea at all. The problem was that the NU Perks Card was taking away their traffic. I must have been the only entrepreneur in history that was trying to get OFF the first page of Google.

After a while, their attorney ended up feeling pretty bad for me and the situation. I wasn't a threat to them. I wasn't even doing anything even close to what they were doing, but I was still infringing on their trademark. I had no choice but to take down the website and stop the business.

The crazy part is that when I first started the business, I had an attorney help me set up the LLC and do the name search. I inquired about trademarking it, and he said, "Nope. Wait until you prove the concept. It's expensive."

That same attorney did me a "favor" by setting up the LLC and name search for free. It turned out that free work isn't the best work because I had NO recourse on him. I used him specifically to prevent something like this from happening, but because I used to be in real estate and we did some business together, he did me a favor.

I even asked Plummeting Profits about trademarking, and they had the same reply—wait until you prove your concept.

Bad advice all around.

And so at this point, I found myself with a business that just failed. There was no way to claw the cards back from people, so at least some money was raised for charity through my earned media approach, and consumers and business owners were happy.

As for me, I was stuck with my new friend Jonny Debt and his $30,000 price tag. Also, let's not forget that in 2008 the bottom fell out of the economy, and credit card interest rates quickly doubled, as did the minimum payments.

So there I was ... totally screwed. It was the moment of truth.

I had a conversation with a bankruptcy attorney, and she said that I would be absolutely crazy to try and come out of this. I had no income, no job, and no way to get a job because I had been doing all of these entrepreneurial adventures.

I looked her in the eye and said, "Winners always find a way to win. I'll figure it out."

So there I went, off to my next adventure.

Remember what I said about finding the blessings in disguise? Well, after that conversation, I found it. My epiphany was two-fold:

Number 1: Traditional Ads

I realized that "traditional" marketing was completely broken. It obviously was a disaster for me, but how many other aspiring entrepreneurs were having their dreams taken away because they used traditional advertising agencies?

I kept thinking ... there has to be a better way. How could business owners accept that losing money in advertising was "normal?" They called it good for "branding" and apparently accepted that this type of advertising was going to lose money. They simply budgeted how much they wanted to lose.

I couldn't even fathom that business would be conducted that way.

Number 2: Online Marketing

Once I had the epiphany that traditional advertising was a losing proposition, I pulled the plug on the wasteful TV commercials and still got as much—if not more—traffic by being on the first page of Google. The traffic and volume were so high that it caught the attention of the other company who then threatened a lawsuit.

What would have happened if I had gotten on the first page of Google for a relevant offer?

My new mission was to embark on an intense pursuit to find the answer to these questions. My goal was to find a better way—to find the solution to the problem of traditional advertising.

I knew that since the economy was in the toilet, there would be lots of people and companies that would love to pay for the solution. So off I went in search of my Holy Grail.

I started Googling Internet marketing and found myself going down about a million rabbit holes. It was the Wild West ... a totally new frontier.

The more I Googled on the topic, the more self-proclaimed "gurus" I found. Everyone was talking about making millions online.

After wading through freight trains of BS and bologna, trying to find out how to market real, legitimate products and services online, I came to the realization that I had to undergo an intense self-education process to truly understand everything about online marketing. I went significantly further into debt to pay for it.

I figured that if I could learn a skill, I would never be upside down like this again. As Maimonides' saying goes, "Give a man a fish and you feed him for a day; teach a man to fish and you feed him for a lifetime."

Unfortunately, after purchasing numerous courses and spending endless hours of study over the course of the next year, I still had not found the solution. I found myself completely overwhelmed and even more broke than when I started since my only income was working part-time selling homes as a REALTOR to keep the lights on.

I eventually hit rock bottom. I was completely down and out and owed $47,500 in credit card debt.

I weighed 213 pounds (I'm 170 today) and started having heart issues—including palpitations and chest pain—and I had high cholesterol. I was still taking it all with a smile, but on the inside it was a complete nuclear meltdown.

Nobody in my life knew this was happening except for me—not my parents, my brother, or my groomsmen in my wedding. I was too embarrassed and didn't want people to try to talk me out of my dreams even further.

So there I was, awake at three in the morning because I could never sleep, and as usual I was watching a webinar about how to market online. Then I saw Eben Pagan's sales video about his mastermind event in Los Angeles.

Eben Pagan is a sought-after thought leader in the online marketing industry who holds mastermind events where like-minded individuals come together to learn and network together. I was totally captivated by his ninety-minute video. He made me feel like he knew everything about me. He was describing my life and challenges better than I could!

He clearly understood WIIFM—what's in it for me.

As I was watching his video, now fully alert and excited, I felt a connection and I knew that I had to be there. I didn't know how I would get there, but I knew that I needed what he offered.

As entrepreneurs, we have to trust our guts at times and have faith—faith to know that once we figure out our purpose in life, the "how" will always reveal itself.

Since I'm the guy who refuses to quit, I called up Eben's support team and finagled a way to put half on my Discover card—literally the last $2,500 of my credit limit. I was now officially 100 percent maxed out on all my cards.

The tough part was that I was still $2,500 shy of the total $5,000 ticket price. I reached out to my good friend Laura, who agreed to go half on it with me since I could bring a guest.

The cost of the course was now covered, but I had absolutely no idea how I was going to find the money to fly from Connecticut to California once every other month as required by the program, but I knew I would figure it out. I had to.

I intensified my real estate focus, and I got a major break when I miraculously sold a home enabling me to pay rent, bills, and have enough left over to get me to LA.

The remaining problem? I didn't have any money for food.

So, I figured, screw it! I was going anyway. I brought a few sandwich bags filled with protein powder.

I figured that everyone attending this event had paid $5,000 to be there, so the networking was going to be incredible. I had to play it cool.

So when we would break for lunch and everyone would go to the hotel restaurant, I would tell folks that I had to make a couple calls. But instead of making calls, I would be mixing up a warm vanilla protein shake in the sink in one of those little hotel glass cups. It was absolutely disgusting, but I would choke down the lumpy mixture and get back downstairs with a smile.

It worked, and all the sacrifice was worth it because this event changed my life in so many ways it's absolutely incredible. I was surrounded by top-level entrepreneurs and learned by observing and networking among them.

I learned about how to "narrow my niche" and how to develop my "ideal target market." I learned enhanced networking skills.

But most importantly, this event offered me a much-needed glimmer of hope.

Unfortunately, that glimmer of hope then met with epic financial disaster. For the first time in my life, I had no way to cover my bills. All my credit cards were maxed out, and I had no cash left and no real estate closings at all in the future.

It was my moment of truth—default for the first time and file bankruptcy or trust my gut and live for my purpose.

After the NU Perks Card failed, it was my MISSION to figure out a solution, and I finally did with online marketing. The challenge was that there were so many ways to advertise online.

So I hit a critical point that all entrepreneurs have to face: be decisive, make a decision, and take urgent action.

My decision was to become a Facebook marketing expert.

So why did I devote an entire chapter to this story?

The reason is simple: I wanted to show you that if you don't have a clearly defined "ideal target market" and advertising that is narrow enough to reach that EXACT "ideal target market," you're going to lose your shirt just like I did.

The marketing takeaway from this tale can be whittled down to six golden nuggets of truth:

1. Earned media (word of mouth) is priceless.

2. Untargeted marketing is dangerous.

3. It is critically important to find your ideal target market.

4. Always trust your gut.

5. Surround yourself with the right people.

6. Never listen when someone says, "We have your best interest in mind."

Chapter 3

The Power of Earned Media and Contests

Nick Unsworth and Valerie Shoopman

-3-

The Power of Earned Media and Contests

The following is a transcript of an actual conversation I had with my mom soon after my epiphany (as I remember it):

"Hi Mom!"

Mama Celeste: "Hey, son, how are you?"

Me: "I'm great, Mama. I'm all fired up because I think I just figured out my purpose."

Mama Celeste: "That's great. What's that?"

Me: "I'm going to be a Facebook marketing expert!"

Mama Celeste: "That's great, Nicky. I'm so happy for you. Now what is that, and are you making any money? I'm worried about you."

It's absolutely true—mothers have a sixth sense.

It has been my great, good fortune to have a mother that loves me no matter what and a father that gave me an unstoppable work ethic. But if I put myself in their shoes, I bet they were constantly worried about me because it looked like I kept trying things that never worked.

As for me … it was all about pulling whatever blessing I could find from each failure.

Oh, and please keep in mind that when I say "failure," I mean that in the most positive manner. A common "blessing" that arose from all my networking marketing failures was that I developed a voracious and insatiable appetite to learn and read, which is kind of ironic since as a kid my parents couldn't get me to read *The Hobbit*—or any other book for that matter—even if they bribed me with an unlimited supply of Chicken McNuggets.

As a result of reading a myriad of entrepreneurial books, I knew that failure was part of the recipe for success, but I also knew that I was at a crossroads and would have to fail forward fast to ultimately find my purpose in life.

And, as you can tell, I got good at failing forward fast.

So I made the decision, and I just told my mother in a telephone conversation on March 22, 2010, that I was going to be a Facebook marketing expert. She responded by giving me the book I mentioned earlier called *The Secret*, which is all about the law of attraction. (I know she gave me the book because she was worried about me.)

This book had such a profound effect on me. It taught me to be aware of the thoughts in my mind. It taught me to stop thinking negative thoughts and to quickly replace them with positive ones. I learned how to manifest my dream life.

I was so immersed in its teachings and such a believer in its power to change my life that I went a little crazy with it and decided to get a tattoo of a cross on my chest with the logo of *The Secret* in the middle of it. I also had the words "Believe 2012" tattooed backwards so that when I brushed my teeth I could clearly read "Believe 2012."

So what did that year signify?

It was my mission to sell a business by the age of thirty. I wanted to sell a business by the end of 2012 before I turned thirty on December 22nd.

You can only imagine how nuts my friends thought I was. They didn't know how deeply in debt I was, but they could tell I had been swinging the bat and hitting nothing but air for quite a while.

When I proclaimed myself to be a Facebook marketing expert to my mom on March 22, 2010, that was also the day I decided to start using my Facebook personal profile! I got dragged onto it in 2007, but I didn't log in or use it until March 2010 when I started my Facebook marketing company.

At this point my life was a total pressure cooker, and I had to quickly come up with over $3,500 to cover my interest payments and $500 rent. So I used the principle of "modeling," which is a fancy way of saying I looked at competitors for ideas for my businesses.

I (and most other online marketers) think in terms of abundance and don't really even think twice about the competition. There's plenty of money out there for all of us.

In my exploration of Facebook marketing experts, I immediately came across Mari Smith. Early on, Mari cornered the market for Facebook marketing. She quickly got a book out, commanded huge speaker fees, and was all over the place online.

Because imitation is the sincerest form of flattery, I made my brand color blue since hers was turquoise. Since she had a brand logo with an "M" in it for Mari, I made mine "NU."

I wish I had been a little more creative at the time because I was modeling Mari a little too closely, but Mari, who also believes in abundance, was OK with it. It helped that I was one of her customers too! We even became good friends, and she featured me in one of her books back in 2011.

The point is that, as an entrepreneur, you can't get stuck and waste valuable time on minor issues. Imperfect action is going to trump sitting on your hands thinking about what to do next every single time.

Stagnation to an entrepreneur is as deadly as a silver bullet to a vampire.

As a man of action, I ran to the local Staples and printed business cards with the new blue brand I had just created. I then went headfirst into local networking meetings as if I had just been shot from a cannon!

Now mind you ... I had no formal expertise and hadn't actually used Facebook for more than a month either.

BUT

I got some amazing advice from Eric Goldstein, an ol' buddy: "You can be an expert as long as you know more than the person you're coaching."

The local market didn't know anything about Facebook marketing, and I had just spent more than $20,000 on courses and seminars. All the courses and books about online marketing gave me the confidence I needed to tell potential clients that I could help them with their Facebook marketing and help them get customers during these tough economic times.

Now, in those days, most local businesses were totally unfamiliar with Facebook marketing and how it would benefit them. So I thought back to the marketing basics that I learned from Eben Pagan:

Who is your target market?

Local business owners.

What is their biggest frustration or challenge?

Traditional marketing is not working for them. They are no longer able to put an ad in the yellow pages and get business. Referral business is no longer enough to sustain them through an economic downturn.

WIIFM: What's in it for them?

You see, this was what I needed to figure out. Why would they want to talk to me? Many of them didn't even realize they needed me yet.

So I created what's called a lead magnet. A lead magnet is something you create that adds value for your target market. Its purpose is to solve a challenge or frustration they have.

Since local small businesses, such as restaurants, REALTORS, and chiropractors, were all suffering for business, I wanted to help the owners solve the problem by helping them attract new customers using Facebook marketing.

So my WIIFM lead magnet was a sixty-minute complimentary consultation that I gave away. I also promised a two-page Facebook marketing plan as well.

The lead magnet was critical because if I just went around talking about Facebook marketing, it wasn't enough. I had to give them a reason to talk to me one-on-one, and at the same time, I had to evidence the value of my business model.

This concept is universal and applicable to all businesses, including yours. You NEED a lead magnet to survive and prosper online. Period!

The approach I took in my initial outreach by phone was to ask them questions about their current marketing approach and explain why traditional marketing wasn't working and why it was costing them money to no discernible benefit. I would then ask questions about what they were doing on social media, and the almost universal response was "nothing." Many of them had absolutely no idea what social media even was.

I would then present my lead magnet, a two-page tailored Facebook marketing plan that explained how this approach would attract additional business. My plan was consistent: they needed to get a Facebook business page and then get reviews.

Local business owners didn't understand Facebook marketing at the time, but they did understand word-of-mouth marketing. You know, that thing called "earned media."

It is important for you to understand the Facebook environment and the psychology associated with its use.

I'm going to assume that you have a personal profile and are currently using it socially, but if you're not, please put this book down and head to www.facebook.com. Create a free account for yourself so that you will better understand what I am trying to relate.

Simply put, people are using Facebook to easily communicate with friends and family. They are sharing what's happening in their lives by posting text, photos, videos, and attachments, and in return they are receiving responses and feedback that enables them to see what's happening in the lives of their friends and family. It is the most elevated form of social connectivity and interaction presently available, which explains its success and popularity.

For the most part, people are not on Facebook looking for solutions to their problems. That's really what Google is for ... answers to questions. So when you consider the Facebook environment, think of it more like a party.

Imagine how annoying it would be if you had a dinner party and someone you didn't know came in and started relentlessly pitching you and all your dinner guests their products and services. How would that make everyone feel?

You would throw the uninvited guest out, and you'll get thrown off Facebook too if you lead with selling first. This is precisely why it's key for you to tap into earned media, the old word of mouth. People trust the recommendations of their friends and family and distrust advertisers they don't know.

As we learned in the last chapter, earned media is all about other people sharing positive things about you or your company. The following is my playbook to apply this strategy for local businesses:

Step 1: Set up a Facebook business page.

www.facebook.com/page

Step 2: Optimize the Facebook business page.

Be sure to add a timeline cover that clearly speaks to what your target market wants and desires. It's also ideal to have a personal brand so that you can truly "connect" with others as a real person as opposed to a company.

Example: I actually have a Facebook business page that is my name, Nick Unsworth. You can go to www.NicksFanPage.com to have a look.

It helps if you imagine your timeline cover as a billboard on a major highway and ask yourself this question: would someone speeding by understand what you do if they glanced at it for a split second while they're going 75 mph?

It's got to be obvious.

At this point in my career, my timeline cover clearly stated: "Facebook Marketing Expert that helps local businesses get customers."

It was clear who I was, who I served, and how I served them.

Once you establish that, you then want to write a clean and simple description of what you do and complete the "about" section in its entirety. Adding your contact info and website addresses are key.

Since Facebook business pages rank well on Google Search, it is important to recognize that fact and realize that what you write is searchable. Keep that in mind if you are going to add keywords into it. You may even pick up some search traffic on Facebook as well.

In my case, my Facebook page is the second search result when someone Googles "Nick Unsworth."

Step 3: Create "wow" customer experiences.

To create word of mouth in your business, you have to over deliver with your customers to give them something to talk about with others. Give your customers a reason to share amazing things about you to their network of contacts on Facebook. I highly recommend the philosophy of under promising and over delivering to create "unexpected bonuses."

As an example: If someone purchases an online training course from me, they will receive a phone call and an e-mail follow-up. In those communications, we always give them an unexpected bonus to create a "wow" experience, something special that's over and above. So if they purchased a course from me, I would throw in an additional course as an unexpected bonus.

Step 4: Ask them to share why they purchased your product with others.

After a customer makes a purchase, we always follow up with a welcome phone call and an e-mail in which we ask one simple question: Would you mind sharing why you purchased xyz?

When they respond to share their excitement for our product or service, we then reply to thank them and to politely ask if they would mind sharing what they said on Facebook. Once they do—BA-BAM! Viral word of mouth begins.

When someone buys a course and then shares their experience on Facebook, it goes something like this:

"I'm so fired up for Nick Unsworth's *Facebook Advertising A to Z* course. I purchased it so that I can learn how to get customers for my xyz business. I'm so looking forward to diving into the training!"

People associate with people that are like them. So if an entrepreneur buys my Facebook Ads A to Z course, the odds are that they have other friends that are entrepreneurial as well that would also see the value in the course. Now, we know that not all their Facebook friends will see it, but the folks they interact with on Facebook are likely to see it in their newsfeeds.

Simply put, Facebook's algorithm typically shares a user's content with those over whom they have influence. What's great about that is that it's coming from a trusted source ... their friend.

So, to have an excellent earned media campaign, you have to start by creating a "wow" experience for your clients, and then you have to ask them to share it.

Asking for referrals is actually the same process.

The interesting thing about the classic manner of asking for referrals is that it's oftentimes awkward and uncomfortable, and then, even when you get them, you may get only one or two. That conversation is one-to-one.

The Facebook earned media strategy is actually one-to-many and far less awkward and intrusive. One person (your customer on Facebook) can share their buying experience with you to their entire list of Facebook friends with a simple click of a button.

You can ask your new customer to share why they purchased from you when you're face-to-face (or at point of sale as some people say). You can also automate that process with a simple autoresponder e-mail that is automatically sent to your new customer after they purchase online, which creates an automated workflow that will help you consistently generate online earned media.

Just keep in mind that when you ask them to share their experience, you want to also be sure to ask them to "tag" you on Facebook so that you're aware of it. Tagging also allows their friends to click on your Facebook business page that is sitting right there amongst the text they've written in the status update sharing why they purchased your product. It makes it very easy for their friends to connect with you if they too are interested in purchasing your product or service.

The nice thing is that when this happens, others that are interested will often respond in the comments section asking questions. That is where it's key for you to chime in and answer any of their friends' questions, which further positions you as the expert and makes it easy to identify prospects.

Step 5: Follow up and ask your customers to "Share with us why you love ...."

Up to this point we have only followed up to ask them to share "why" they purchased. That buying excitement is marketing gold on Facebook.

The next step is to follow up after they have consumed your products or service. This is not only excellent customer service, but it also is a great touch point to then ask the golden question: "Tell us why you love xyz."

Again, you can call or automatically set your e-mail to reach out to your customers, let's say thirty days after the sale, to ask them why they love xyz product. When they respond, you can ask them to share it on Facebook in the form of a status update or even a "review."

Folks have the ability to write reviews on local Facebook pages. They choose from a multiple star rating and then click "submit," and that story has the ability to be shared with their friends in the newsfeed. When others share a five-star review about your products / services, that is incredibly powerful earned media for their friends to see.

Step 6: You can leverage the "review" strategy with contests.

When I was at Eben Pagan's event in 2009, I met Scott who recently sold a business and started a huge project for the insurance industry. Scott and I became good friends while at the event learning Internet marketing, and his company became my first five-figure contract, which then led into my first six-figure contract. The majority of the work I did for them revolved around leveraging this review strategy with local insurance agents all over the country.

Local insurance agents who sell property and casualty insurance live off referrals, but it was old school one-on-one. When I explained how we could leverage reviews from their customers and turn those reviews into viral word of mouth via Facebook marketing, they immediately saw its promise. They understood referrals and loved that we could turn them into viral word of mouth on Facebook through a concept called the review contest strategy.

What I have explained thus far is a process to routinely ask for reviews and referrals as you do business. What I'm about to share is a contest strategy where you ask ALL your customers to write a review during a set period of time during a contest.

With Scott's company, we would have the insurance agent set the contest start and end date, which was ideally three weeks. They would then choose a contest prize that had a value of $300 to $500. We tested everything from gift certificates to TVs to iPads. We found that iPads (or now iPad minis) worked the best.

So once you establish your contest prize that fits your market, you reach out via e-mail to your entire target market database of, in this example, insurance agents and explain that you're doing a "referral contest." The purpose of the e-mail is to get the person to click on a link that sends them to a website page that explains how the contest works.

It's ideal to have a simple headline at the top, such as "NJU Insurance Referral Contest."

From there, include a video that:

- Welcomes and thanks them for their business

- Lets them know that your business thrives off referrals from customers

- Defines what a great referral is for you

- Tells them about the steps they have to take to enter the contest

- Calls them to action to do the steps now

- Tells them that the contest ends on X date

Step 1: Click here to write a review.

You want to link this to your Facebook page so that when they write a review, you can let them know that they got one "entry" to the sweepstakes (a.k.a. a raffle) to win the iPad.

Step 2: Receive five entries for EVERY referral that you send over.

This rewards your customers for actually sending over a referral. In your video, you want to explain what a perfect referral looks like and how they can connect them with you. Having your existing customer make an e-mail introduction is often the most efficient way to send over a referral.

Step 3: Receive ten entries when you purchase a new policy.

This is to encourage the new referrals your customers send over to take action within the contest period and make a buying decision and then reward them for doing so. In this example, it's purchasing a policy. For your business it can be buying your product / service.

Once you start the referral contest, it's key to routinely post about it on Facebook as well as provide a status update to let your fans' "likes" know about it. You definitely need to accompany these updates with consistent e-mail updates as well.

What's critical to this strategy is that instead of talking about insurance on an insurance Facebook page, we're actually talking about a contest instead and sharing updates and milestones.

The following are examples of some status updates:

"We're so excited to kick off our NJU Insurance referral contest where we're giving away an iPad this month. Simply click on xyz.com to learn how you can enter."

"We're so grateful for all the reviews and referrals that our fans have sent over. We grow our business through word of mouth, and we can't thank you enough!"

Status update: Screen capture (take a picture) and share reviews to solicit additional business external to the target market.

This acts as social proof for your fans. You will inevitably have folks that like your Facebook business page but haven't taken action yet to make purchase from you. When they see others buying and see the reviews that read like testimonials, it will help make others feel comfortable to also purchase through you.

As the contest draws closer to the end date, it's super important to let everyone know via status updates and e-mail that there are only five days left to enter. Only three days left to enter, etc. This creates urgency, and urgency is one of the most powerful motivators in marketing.

You may also want to let people know that there are only, for example, eighty-five entries, so their odds of winning are great.

Once the contest concludes, you manually look at all the reviews that you received and give one entry for each of them. I recommend typing the person's name and how many entries they accumulated on an Excel spreadsheet.

Then, add in the additional entries they received through the contest for referrals as well as any folks that have purchased your products and services as well.

Once you've tallied all the data on a simple Excel spreadsheet, or on paper for that matter, you can then cut them up into little raffle tickets so that you can pull the winner out of a hat or fish bowl ... whatever you prefer. We found that making a video of you choosing the winner and posting it creates a level of transparency that your Facebook fans will love.

Once you pick the winning raffle ticket out of the fish bowl, you then e-mail and share status updates of the results.

Important note: Be sure to review Facebook's promotion guidelines and check with sweepstakes regulations in your state to make sure you're in compliance. It's also very important to have your contest rules stated on the bottom of the contest page as well.

This review contest strategy worked so well that we ended up working with a multi- billion dollar insurance carrier to scale up this approach nationwide for their local insurance agents. We taught their agents in online webinars how to set up their contests, and the results were absolutely incredible. A local insurance agent could get anywhere from five to thirty-five new insurance policies within three weeks by using the referral contest strategy.

I share this strategy using insurance agents as the example because if insurance agents can do it ... you can too! (This comment is not intended to be a slight against insurance agents; it's just that everyone used to think marketing insurance on Facebook was hopeless.)

The reason this strategy works so well is simple: it's as easy as getting other people to want to share positive stories about you or your company to their friends on Facebook.

I can personally attest that the review contest approach is a winning and profitable strategy because it **Got Me Out of Debt—Fast!** (As you will recall, when I started the Facebook marketing business, I was $50,000 in debt and on the verge of personal financial collapse.)

I shared this very strategy in dozens upon dozens of free consultations with local business owners, and invariably each owner would ask, "Nick, can you help me implement this? I'm just too busy."

I would then cook up a quick proposal and get to work. Since I added value first with my free sixty-minute consultation and then added value with my two-page Facebook marketing plan, I was able to quickly generate cash flow to cover my expenses.

In the first month, I had to cover $3,500 to pay my bills. I ended up making just a hair over $5,000. This created much-needed progress, and progress in your business usually translates to momentum. Business momentum is similar to an athlete getting into the "zone." It's a flow state that allows you to be at your best.

The momentum of being able to pay my bills inspired confidence, and I took that to the next level. I kept "networking up" and raising my prices as I created more value for my customers.

As an example, if I could create $2,500 in revenue for an insurance agent within sixty days, I could charge $1,000 for that. The agent, who sees that this is quite a bit better than going to an advertising company and spending $30,000 to make back $280 of gross revenue, has no complaints.

Photo-Sharing Strategy:

Another incredible way to generate powerful word of mouth for your business on Facebook is by leveraging photos.

Within the first ninety days of my business, while I was cranking away in the local market, I decided to also turn my attention to real estate. I started with one REALTOR and soon got them five-figure results. I then leveraged that to get into one of the top five real estate brokerages in the United States.

One of the most effective strategies I developed and implemented was the photo-sharing strategy that also tapped into earned media. Did you know that Facebook is the largest photo-sharing network in the world?

Here's how it worked and how you can take this idea and incorporate it into your business:

When a REALTOR or buyer's agent sells a home, they always do a final walkthrough on the day of closing, which is an exciting time for the buyer. Because of this, I suggested a policy of having the REALTOR try to take a photo of the client in front of their brand-new home that was readily accepted.

They would then ask permission of the buyers by saying something like, "OK, Travis and Laura, once we finalize the closing, do you mind if I share this photo on Facebook?" Nine out of ten times the buyers would say yes.

The agent would then post the photo on Facebook as a status update and tag the new homeowners. This effectively breaks the news to the buyers' friends and family members on Facebook.

The agent would then write in the description something like this:

"Travis and Laura, it was so great working with you throughout the home-buying process, and I wish you many, many years of happiness in your beautiful new home. If you should ever need anything—a free market analysis, a recommendation for a contractor—or if you have any other questions, please don't hesitate to call me at 555-751-0285. E-mail also works well agent@xyzemailaddress.com."

The post then ends up in the newsfeed of the buyers' friends and family, and it goes viral because it's such a big moment in life. Their friends and family see the news, like the photo, and comment to say congratulations.

When the buyers get back on Facebook, they see all the action on the photo status update of their new home. They always respond with something amazing to say about the buying experience because of the extra nice description the agent wrote on the photo. That description led the buyers to reply with some incredibly complimentary words about the agent in the comments.

And presto!

There you have it ... positive words about the agent amongst a status update where many of their friends and family have commented. Their response would act like a powerful testimonial that would create sales leads for the agent.

This strategy worked exceptionally well for the first-time homebuyer market because, at that age, many of their friends would be interested in buying a home as well. I mean, who better to call than the agent about whom the buyers just spoke so favorably?

This simple photo-sharing strategy created so much new business for so many agents that this became standard practice when selling a home. It quickly became part of their home-selling system that would perpetually create more leads after each sale.

So my question to you is this: how can you leverage the photo-sharing strategy in YOUR business?

Nick Unsworth and Valerie Shoopman

Chapter 4

How to Attract Ideal Customers with a Lead Magnet and Facebook Marketing Funnel

Nick Unsworth and Valerie Shoopman

-4-

How to Attract Ideal Customers with a Lead Magnet and Facebook Marketing Funnel

As I was cranking away, working with local businesses such as REALTORS, insurance agents, restaurants, chiropractors, etc., I decided to try some strategies to grow my Facebook business page into other profitable avenues. I figured that if I wanted to be able to get to larger markets and bigger companies, I needed to look the part. I needed to go from 810 Facebook likes to more than 10,000.

That's when I decided to turn my attention to testing Facebook via a Facebook marketing funnel with a lead magnet.

What exactly is a lead magnet?

A lead magnet is something of value used to attract your ideal target market.

A lead magnet is often found to be the solution to a problem that your market has. The key ingredient for me as a Facebook marketer is that for your prospects to obtain your value add lead magnet, they have to exchange information to get your solution.

For example: If my target market is struggling with sales because traditional marketing no longer works for them, then a great lead magnet would offer the solution to that problem.

In this case, sharing free tips on how to generate sales using Facebook marketing would be a great solution. For them to get the solution, they would need to enter their e-mail address to get access to the free report, webinar, or free consultation.

A lead magnet works because you first have to give to them on Facebook and add value. This builds your relationship with your prospects and establishes a basis of trust so that they then *want* to buy your products and services. This is the key differentiator from traditional "push" marketing in which you push your marketing message upon prospects and hope that they take you up on it.

What are the benefits of using a lead magnet in your marketing?

The first benefit is that it attracts your ideal prospects to you and then captures their information so that you create a lead.

Many refer to this as building your e-mail list, which is the backbone of building a sustainable business. You have to have a pipeline of prospects at all times, and when you consistently build your e-mail list, you can enjoy a long-term sustainable flow of new customers to your business.

The lead magnet conversion totem pole:

When deciding what your lead magnet will be, it's important to know how your intended magnet(s) will perform as it relates to turning leads into paying customers and raving fans. A lead magnet can be a free value add phone consultation, informational webinar, video training, coupon, free report, or even a contest entry.

I listed these in order of highest converting to lowest converting, in other words, the percentage of people that obtain your lead magnet and then go on and become a paying customer.

One-on-One, Face-to-Face: # 1

If you developed and introduced a lead magnet that you advertised on Facebook in your local market to arrange for a free, in-person consultation, this strategy would have the highest likelihood of conversions.

Face-to-face meetings with your prospects will give you the ability to add value in person and afford you the opportunity to then make them an offer to purchase your products and services. Belly-to-belly (also known as face-to-face) is always going to give you the highest probability of closing a sale.

One-on-One Virtual:

If you were to give away a free consultation that was delivered virtually, it would also convert well but not as well as face-to-face because they can only hear you—they can't physically see you in person.

One-to-Many in Person:

For example, you could give away a free ticket to an in-person workshop. We tested this out for a home-buying seminar in real estate in the local market with great success.

One-to-Many Virtual:

A live webinar, or a live stream like a Google Hangout, gives you the ability to build rapport live, and they can hear your voice and even see you over a webcam. This is an incredible way to scale your business and create conversions. This is my favorite approach because it is more scalable. You're able to leverage your time more effectively. (Please note that the rate of conversions—your probability of making sales—is higher in the above three strategies.)

This is the primary method that we have used with our business and our clients to scale from six- to seven-figure revenue.

Later in the book, Valerie Shoopman will walk you through a step-by-step process on how to run ads to a webinar lead magnet.

Video Series:

When the person opts in, they receive a series of videos in which you add value on a topic applicable to them and solve a problem their target market has.

Audio Recording:

This is much like a video series, but is simply the audio.

Free report:

After entering their e-mail address, your prospect receives an informational free report that adds value.

What is a Facebook marketing funnel?

A Facebook marketing funnel has a wide mouth at the top where the client for whom you are developing your lead magnet enters their prospects. They then agree to commit with you to obtain the lead magnet, which creates an exchange of information and captures the leads.

From there, your Facebook marketing funnel follows up to continue to add value for the prospect and convert them into a buyer—and then a raving fan that sends in referrals.

Valerie will break down the advanced mechanics later in this book, so stay tuned!

Facebook contest lead magnet and marketing funnel:

As I related earlier, I purchased thousands of dollars' worth of courses on Facebook marketing, and I decided to test the iPad contest strategy that I learned about in one of the courses for my business. I followed the instructions to the letter.

This particular course said to create a Facebook landing tab that lives inside your Facebook business page. You can use www.leadpages.net to do this.

The page said "iPad Giveaway" at the top and then had a video explaining how it worked. It was quite simple. Anyone who entered their e-mail address would enter to win the iPad. It worked much like a sweepstakes or raffle.

From there, I was instructed to use a picture of a woman holding an iPad as a right side Facebook ad. I thought this was a little odd since I'm a guy, but I figured I would test it as it was taught in the course.

I created the ad copy that said, "Click here to enter to win an iPad." I then targeted a broad list of entrepreneurs.

The results?

It completely flopped! I was spending over $10 on Facebook ads to get just one person to enter their e-mail. I quickly flashed back to my advertising days with the NU

Perks Card and decided to turn it off immediately and reevaluate.

I then considered the Facebook environment and decided to do it my way. I figured that Facebook is all about connections and relationships. If you think about building an audience on Facebook, it's key to be transparent and authentic.

So I swapped out the picture of the gorgeous blond woman and replaced it with a selfie I took of myself holding an iPad. I then looked at the original written copy and thought that it was awfully cheesy to say, "Click here to enter to win an iPad" because it seemed a little salesy and spammy.

I replaced that old copy with "What do you think of my new Facebook page!?"

What's interesting is that I was simply being friendly. I was being me. It was personal and I asked a question.

The results were absolutely staggering!

I went from paying more than $10 per e-mail opt-in to paying 10 cents per e-mail opt-in. In addition, close to 50 percent of all the people that opted in with their e-mail address were also choosing to "like" my page.

I also narrowed my targeting on the Facebook advertising platform and chose to advertise to chief marketing officers. I figured that since it was 2010 and there was so much buzz about Facebook marketing, there had to be a ton of companies trying to figure it out. Not only did I quickly grow the likes on my page and e-mail list, but I was also creating incredible brand positioning.

When you run ads on Facebook and you're an aspiring coach, speaker, expert, or online marketer, those that see your ads everywhere will quickly perceive you to have authority. This was evident when an unknown caller dialed my number.

Me: "Hi! This is Nick!"

Quincy: "Hey, Nick! Oh, wow, I'm so glad I could catch you directly. I thought maybe I would end up speaking to your receptionist first."

Me (bewildered): "Oh … well, you know … I still like to answer calls at times."

Quincy: "So I'm running a large technology conference in Honolulu later this year and was looking at what you're doing on Facebook, and I'm so impressed. I was calling to ask you to be a keynote speaker."

Me (even more shocked): "That sounds great, Quincy. What are the details, and how much are you paying for the keynote?" (I still love thinking about the guts I had to say that.)

Quincy: "Well, we don't have a huge budget, but we can pay a $1,500 fee, plus we can cover all your travel expenses."

Me: "I've been dying to get to Hawaii and would be honored, Quincy."

Quincy: "OK, well, send me your media kit and let's get the ball rolling."

Me: "Sure thing! I'll do it right away. Cheers!"

From there, I frantically Googled, "What's a media kit?"

Just imagine for a second the brand positioning that my Facebook ads created. I was sitting there in my tiny second bedroom, living in a rough part of town, digging my way out of $50,000 of debt, yet Quincy perceived me to be an expert worthy enough to be a keynote speaker.

This is exactly when I learned that I had to go toward my fear. (You may remember I mentioned earlier that I had a fear of public speaking.) After failing forward fast and overcoming obstacles two at a time, I realized that when I experienced fear, I could reframe it and harness the power for good.

I started to think that the fear I experienced was an indicator that must mean that I was about to grow ... a lot! So I faced my fear. Off I went to be a keynote speaker, and my world started changing incredibly fast.

Again, the more progress I created, the more momentum I stepped into.

The Facebook Like Campaign – How to Get Likes for Less than 10 cents:

In addition to the iPad contest, I decided to reinvest business profits into an advertising campaign to grow my likes and get them past 10,000. I knew that the more likes I had, the more social proof it would create.

When you have more than 10,000 likes, it creates instant credibility for your prospects. This translates into all kinds of benefits for your business—everything from increasing your prices, speaking engagements, and extending your reach on Facebook.

I'm going to share with you an equation I created for a like campaign that will crush.

Title your right-hand side Facebook ad: "(Your Industry) Fan?"

"Click 'LIKE' if you LOVE (industry name)."

Example:

Business Fan?

"Click 'LIKE' if you love social media."

Targeting: Next, go into the Facebook advertising editor and narrow your targeting to the perfect prospect that would LOVE the industry that you're referring to.

In my case, I targeted people who "like" the top social media marketing fan pages. I expected great results because I was targeting people that I know LOVE social media. I knew that when they saw the ad, they would not resist clicking the like button associated with my ad on the right-hand side.

In a nutshell, the reason the above two Facebook advertising strategies work so well is that Facebook rewards you for having ads that people "want" to click on. Simply put, when your ad has a high click-through rate (CTR), which means a high percentage of the people who saw the ad clicked on it, it will reduce your ad costs or cost per click (CPC).

If you just think about making your ads friendly as opposed to salesy, you're going to drive down your ad costs. This strategy alone allowed me to get Facebook business page likes for less than 10 cents each, and I quickly got my page past 10,000 likes. The brand positioning and authority it created was absolutely incredible.

I quickly started getting even more speaking engagements, was asked to write chapters in Facebook marketing books, and was getting inquiries for me to consult with large companies faster than I could keep up.

So my business grew and evolved, and you're not going to believe what happened next!

Nick Unsworth and Valerie Shoopman

Chapter 5

Narrow Your Niche, Grow Rich, and Have a Purpose-Driven Business

Nick Unsworth and Valerie Shoopman

-5-

Narrow Your Niche, Grow Rich, and Have a Purpose-Driven Business

Tuesday, January 1, 2012.

So there I was, looking in the mirror at my tattoo of a cross with "Believe 2012" written backwards on my chest. I was reflecting on the absolutely incredible ride that I had been on for the past two years as a Facebook marketing expert.

I had gone from eating protein mix out of a sandwich bag at an event because I was $50,000 in debt to making a six-figure annual net income with no debt.

I was incredibly proud of the hard work that I had done—proud of paying off my debt and finally getting my career on track and proud of my mission to help business owners actually get a positive return on investment on their Facebook advertising.

But there was one thing left.

I had the goal of selling a business by the end of 2012.

It's what I had been dreaming of for years. Ever since I got the tattoo, I would wake up in the morning and read a letter that I wrote to myself of what it would feel like after I sold a business.

I was obsessed with the mission. Selling a business by the end of 2012 symbolized me "making it" it as an entrepreneur. It was the ultimate goal that pulled me through challenge after challenge. It was also the reason I sacrificed taking an actual vacation for seven years. I sacrificed much of my twenties in pursuit of this dream.

I was certain that selling a business would bring me an absolute abundance of happiness. It could be compared to daydreaming about how amazing life will be after you retire.

So, as I stood in front of the mirror, I started thinking of ways to make it happen. I had to make it happen. I couldn't stand the thought of having this goal on my chest and letting myself down. Fortunately, with all of this hard work, my business was totally kicking butt. I had more clients than I could handle.

I had a six-figure client for whom I was the social media director for a huge insurance marketing project, and it was taking off. They were aggressively raising money and building out their team. We had created so much success for their local insurance agents that I was one of their top consultants.

My business was soaring, and I couldn't help but look at my six-figure contract with them and start to second-guess it. A contract worth $100,000 per year was a lot of money and a steady revenue flow for me, but what about opportunity cost? At this point, I had been putting more than half my time and energy into this one client alone. What other profitable opportunities was I forsaking as a result?

That's when I decided to have a candid conversation with my client about reducing my hours and pay so that I could focus on growing my business. At the time, I didn't have all the dots connected regarding my goal. I genuinely wanted to just invest more time into my own company.

What happened next was nothing short of a miracle—something out of a movie. After our conversation they came back to me and said, "What if we acquired your company?"

Their mergers and acquisitions guy mentioned that they could build a support system around me that would allow me to flourish and focus on doing the parts of the business that I truly love.

I was overcome with joy just thinking about the possibilities. I started thinking about a life where I could have a team to handle aspects of the business that I didn't enjoy so that I could focus on applying my strengths. It all sounded amazing, so I jumped at the opportunity and explored the conversation. What I loved about them was that we shared the same values. I trusted them like family.

The negotiation process was like nothing I had ever experienced before. They had a mergers and acquisitions team that had literally done over a billion dollars of transactions. I quickly realized that I was completely out of my league and was opening myself up for major risk. I sought counsel to protect myself, and the process got more and more intense.

We would come up with terms, and then the lawyers would come back with a term sheet that was more than fifty pages long. It was like reading Japanese. As the intensity grew, so did the legal fees. Every time my attorney reviewed the exhaustive term sheet it would take a $5,000 bite out of my savings.

We went back and forth for months until finally settling on a number. I would sell the majority of my company to them, and we would then start a new division that I would run. That new company would then service their large insurance project, which would provide a constant revenue flow. I wasn't crazy about doing the work in insurance, but I WAS crazy about selling my business—almost too crazy.

At the end of the grueling process, I ended up with 37.5 percent of the new company and would receive my compensation for the sale of my assets through an "earn out." This meant that for two years I would stay on as the CEO and earn a monthly installment payment for the assets and intellectual property I was bringing into the new company. This multiple six-figure payout was more money than I had ever made, and I took the deal.

We serviced the insurance industry and also sold social media marketing coaching programs. In the process, we had some significant ups and downs, and I found myself outside my comfort zone on a daily basis.

The challenge arose when we decided to base much of the business on a product launch that, although it hit high six-figure revenues, carried huge expenses for us. Due to the fact that we didn't hit our net profit numbers, my partners ended up shifting the focus of the business back to the insurance industry. One thing I learned was that when you change your plan, you start back at square one each time.

We ended up in a constant tug-of-war about who our "ideal" target market was. We would flip-flop between serving the insurance industry and coaching entrepreneurs. This put incredible strain on the business because to be successful, you have to be EXCELLENT at something. Every business needs a core focus—a flagship product, something that you can rinse and repeat, something with which you can gain efficiency.

As we trudged on, we found ourselves trying to cater to B2B (business to business) and B2C (business to consumer) at the same time, as well as targeting different markets within each. This was completely contrary to the one thing that I would like to drive home in this book and that is the importance of your "ideal" target market.

All this floundering around put such massive financial stress on the business that I found myself in a tough spot and decided to move across the country to San Diego. Part of my dream of selling a business was the vision of having a home on the ocean, so I made it happen. I was balancing the excitement of selling my business, starting a new one, going through a significant breakup, and moving across the country. It was a lot.

And then came the moment that changed everything:

After months of working in the new company as the CEO, I arrived in sunny San Diego. I took the money I made from selling my company and got my dream home right on the water in Pacific Beach San Diego.

I purchased gorgeous "things" to furnish my new home— my first bedroom set, decent pots and pans, a nice leather couch, and the list goes on and on. I'll never forget the night when I finally had everything moved into my new place. I grabbed a beer to celebrate and went onto the balcony overlooking the water.

I stood there, a beer in my hand, staring out over the water, expecting to feel joy, accomplishment, and happiness. Instead, what I felt was the deepest feeling of sadness I've ever experienced in my entire life. I was totally alone, and I felt like everything I had been dreaming of for so many years had been a total lie.

I sold my baby and ended up with a minority stake in a company that was no longer aligned with my purpose and passion in life. I felt like I had sold out and replaced my business that I loved with a job. I realized that the concept of "selling a business" was a total illusion. This was NOT at all what I expected.

So why on earth am I sharing this in a Facebook marketing book?

The reason is simple:

We spend the majority of our lives working. We spend more time working than we do with friends, family, and loved ones.

I realized at that moment on the balcony that if you don't have purpose or meaning in your life, and if you don't love what you do for work, no amount of money will ever make you happy.

That's when I had a total epiphany or "ah-ha" moment.

Life is truly about being happy. Much of our sense of fulfillment and purpose comes from our life's work, and that's where the majority of our time goes.

At that moment I drew a line in the sand and decided to resign as CEO and forgo much of the money that I would have made to pursue true happiness. I figured I would simply create a business where I love what I do for work every single day. My goal was to simply enjoy the day-to-day journey as opposed to waiting for some false hope at the end destination.

Overall, I wanted to be on a journey worth living. Life is way too short to wait until the sale of a business or retirement to be happy.

Once I realized this, I was off to the races to figure out what came next. Fortunately, I met my very good friend Shanda Sumpter at my housewarming party. She was glowing like a Christmas tree with a smile that was ear to ear. Something was so different—she was clearly happy on a level that I'd actually never seen in anyone before.

I was so curious about what on earth she was doing. As we spoke, I learned that she was a business coach and had a multimillion-dollar business where she was helping others live their dreams and creating success stories. She takes one week off per month, travels the world, and most importantly, she enjoys the journey every step of the way.

I asked, "So how on earth did you create this lifestyle for yourself?"

Shanda: "I have a coach."

Why Everyone Needs a Coach:

"A coach!?" I said in complete bewilderment. I was thinking to myself, *That's all it takes—hiring a freaking coach?*

Shanda was kind enough to afford me a deep look into her business and her experience with her coach and the benefits she provided. I immediately realized I needed one as well.

I bombarded Shanda's coach with all the reasons she should take me on as a client, a position that would require me to pay her $36,000 a year to be coached. To this day this decision stands out as the best investment I've ever made in my life.

We worked together to create a life and business that I love.

Every Business Needs Purpose:

Have you ever been at a place in your life where you've felt like there are a million directions you could go—a fork in the road, if you will? Well, I was a bit of a hot mess after all of this, and she helped me realize that when you love what you do for work, the money will follow. Shoot, an amazing life will follow.

But to get there, your business has to have purpose.

So she asked me a question that rattled my cage: "What f-ing pisses you off?"

Me: "Um ... I dunno. I'm a pretty non-confrontational kind of guy."

Coach: "What's the movement you want to start?"

Me: "I've never really thought about that."

Coach: "What's your stance in life?"

These questions created an absolute tornado of emotions and confusion until I finally got the point.

You see, incredible businesses and lives are driven by something bigger than themselves. They're driven by a vision and a purpose that are much more significant than just making money.

So after a series of calls and questions, I totally cracked it. I figured out my purpose in life. Sounds a bit crazy, right, the purpose of my life? But I've got to tell you, when you shift your business focus onto one purpose and drill down, everything will change. Your marketing, your conversions, your cash flow, your impact on this world, and your general level of happiness and well-being will change.

Since then I've taken this entire experience and boiled it down to a process that I call the "Three S's." By going through this exercise, you too can shift your business or career to have greater meaning and impact.

Figuring this out will set your Facebook marketing on fire, and you'll never have to worry about money again.

You'll start to measure your success in terms of how many people you serve and how much impact you make. Money won't be the focus, but the irony is that when you love what you do and you're rooted in your mission, it will find a way to flow to you like never before.

"Three S's":

"What's your Story?"

So often our background story leaves clues. The things we experience in life that serve as breadcrumbs on the path to finding your true calling. For some, it's leveraging something negative that happened.

Example:

A young alcoholic who ends up in the hospital and almost dies comes back with a whole new lease on life and is now on a mission to help and inspire those around him to get help and claim their life back.

Example:

A person who grew up in the "system" as a foster child becomes an adult with a burning desire to help other foster children.

In my case, I realized that the consistent theme in all my entrepreneurial journeys was that I was always chasing money and opportunity. I had a servant's heart with a need to please and always wanted to give back, but the problem was that I was more focused on the end destination instead of enjoying the journey each and every single day.

I used to think to myself, "I'll sacrifice my twenties and be happy later—after I sell a business." I now live my life in the present moment and focus on being happy each and every single day.

"What's your Stance?"

What do you stand for? What pisses you off? What's your movement? How do you want to be remembered? What's your legacy?

While thinking about my background story, it became clear to me that what pisses me off is when someone spends their life working in a line of work they don't like. It pisses me off to think about all the folks who have a gift inside them that is just waiting to be shared with the world—if they had the guts to explore it. It pisses me off to think about people spending their life working, focused on the end destination, and not enjoying the day-to-day journey.

It was clear to me that my story of sacrificing everything for the false hope of the end destination as opposed to enjoying the journey is what pisses me off. Realizing this helped me formulate my mission to help others live what I call a Life on Fire.

What is a Life on Fire?

It's a life where you love what you do for work. A life based on happiness and giving back to others. A life where you're living up to your true potential and making a difference.

It's important to keep in mind that that's what a Life on Fire looks like to me. Each person has their own definition of a Life on Fire.

A stay-at-home mom's mission could be to give her kids a better life than she had. Maybe that mission stems from hardships she endured as a child.

When you're on a mission and have purpose in business, you'll find that you'll wake up earlier in the morning, eager to go to work. You'll find that you're "inspired" to work each and every day. You'll find that when you face a challenge the size of a mountain, it will appear to you to be only the size of an anthill.

When you're operating your business with purpose, anything is possible and nothing can stop you. There's no obstacle too big.

It's the biggest game changer.

This motivational and mindset alignment will change everything in your marketing as well. It's the difference between struggling to make sales versus attracting sales to you like a high-powered magnet.

There are clues everywhere:

For example, TOMS shoes is a company whose founders' mission is to give a pair of shoes to a child in a developing nation each and every time a pair of shoes is purchased. Their "Stance" is based on the story of the business, and their business growth has been absolutely incredible.

Adam Braun, the founder of "Pencils of Promise," is another great example. Adam took his background story of traveling through Guatemala and seeing firsthand the hardships children face due to the lack of resources available to them for their education and started a charity to build schools in Guatemala and other developing nations. It has been a dramatic success.

These stories are happening over and over, and it's the difference between making a living and truly living a Life on Fire.

"What's your Strategy?"

How can you take your story and stance and turn them into a viable business?

If you're already in business, how can you shift your marketing to reflect your mission?

It's at this point that many entrepreneurs get totally hung up on searching and searching for the answers, desperate for a place to start. The truth of the matter, however, is that the fastest path to success to study is to look where success is already happening.

As an example, look around online and find people or companies that are doing what you would love to do and "model" their business strategy. You can look at three different companies, model aspects of each, and create your perfect company or marketing plan.

For me, once I harnessed my background story and figured out my stance, I then found a couple business strategies that I wanted to model.

Example:

I knew that my business would be 50 percent like Shanda Sumpter's, 25 percent like Joe Polish's (who runs the "Genius Network" that brings high-caliber entrepreneurs together three times per year to collaborate and network), and 25 percent like Marie Forleo's business. (I wanted to model her weekly video show called *Marie TV.*)

I didn't copy them. I modeled strategies from three successful businesses that I admired and blended them into a business suited to my desire for my perfect life and business.

Here's the *Life on Fire Manifesto*:

IF THERE'S SMOKE, THERE'S FIRE.
SOMETIMES YOU JUST NEED THE RIGHT MATCH TO SET YOUR LIFE *ABLAZE.*

AS KIDS, WE DREAMED OF SETTING THE WORLD ON FIRE. OF STANDING OUT AND BEING RICHLY REWARDED.

But for many of us, somewhere along the way that fire got a bucket of ice cold water dumped onto it, stopping it in its tracks.

IT'S WHY SO MANY OF US RELEGATE OURSELVES TO LIVES OF MEDIOCRITY.

WHICH WOULD ALL BE FINE IF THAT YEARNING WENT AWAY. IF WE DIDN'T HAVE A SPARK OF PASSION THAT WAS DYING TO GET OUT.

MOST OF US BELIEVE WE ARE MEANT TO LIVE IN THE DARK.

AND YET...

THERE'S STILL THAT DESIRE.

THERE'S STILL A HOPE THAT THIS LIFE CAN ALLOW US TO MAKE EVERYDAY OF OUR LIVES AN ADVENTURE, A JOURNEY WORTH LIVING.

WE CAN HAVE WHAT IS KNOWN AS A LIFE ON FIRE.
A LIFE WHERE WE PROFIT WILDLY BEYOND OUR WILDEST DREAMS.

WHICH BRINGS YOU TO THE MOMENT OF TRUTH.

If you're still feeling that burning desire for more, than it's time to start paying attention to what those desires are trying to tell you.

 IT'S TIME TO REALIZE THAT IN YOUR HANDS LIES THE SINGLE MATCH THAT CAN SET YOUR LIFE ABLAZE.

IT'S JUST UP TO YOU WHETHER OR NOT **YOU SET FIRE TO YOUR LIFE.**

WELCOME — TO — *Life on Fire*

Narrowing Your Niche, Your Ideal Target Market:

In many cases, you can effectively modify your stance by simply drilling down and narrowing your "ideal" target market. Many people and companies spend so much time working with customers that pay the bills but who may not actually be "ideal" customers.

Example:

My client Chadi is a top-performing coach in the real estate industry. I asked him who his "ideal" target market is.

Chadi: "Women REALTORS between the ages of forty and fifty who are struggling, who don't understand technology, and who are looking to increase their income."

Me: "Is that your 'ideal,' or is that the 'ideal' of those with whom you're currently working?"

Chadi: "Hmm …."

Me: "Chadi, if you could work with anyone, who would that be? Who could you work with that would totally light you up and give you energy, and who would be fun to work with?"

Chadi: "Well, actually, it would be men that are hungry, committed, coachable, and between the ages of twenty-five and thirty-five."

Me: "Man, what a difference! Why don't you shift your marketing to them??"

You see, it's very common for entrepreneurs and service professionals to accept second best. It does not have to be that way, however, and this recognition causes a massive shift that takes place within ourselves when we consciously decide who our truly "ideal" target market is.

When you're working with ideal customers, everything changes. For example, they aren't as price sensitive, and ideal customers have friends like them and refer more ideal customers.

Because I had the epiphany to focus on loving what I do for work and because I had started Life on Fire, I realized exactly who and what lights me up. That one shift started to change everything.

The following are steps to figuring out your ideal target market:

1. Think of the perfect prospect that you would LOVE to work with day in and day out.
2. Write out everything about them in vivid detail: How old are they? Are they male or female, married or single? Do they have kids or no kids? Where do they live? What are their hobbies, interests, career, and income range? What books do they like? What are their favorite TV shows, and most importantly ... what Facebook pages do they "like"?

3. Go on Facebook and find the Facebook pages that your ideal customer would "like." This is going to be incredibly beneficial for your Facebook advertising, which Valerie will teach you later in this book.

The key takeaway is that once you are clear on your ideal target market, you want to then find the Facebook pages that they "like." This research will ultimately lead you to massive success with Facebook advertising.

Nick Unsworth and Valerie Shoopman

Chapter 6

How to Write Your Own Checks with a Webinar Marketing Funnel

Nick Unsworth and Valerie Shoopman

-6-

How to Write Your Own Checks with a Webinar Marketing Funnel

Running my own Facebook ads had been serving me well for years, but after really digging down into my highest and best use, I knew that I could grow faster if I had help.

One lesson I'll never forget is to NEVER outsource all your marketing. Nobody cares like you do, period.

BUT ... after expending all my time and effort with all the entrepreneurs and companies that I was coaching on Facebook marketing, I ended up creating a small army of entrepreneurs that were interested in doing what I was doing for work. Rather than fear the competition that I was creating, I embraced it instead and started teaching others how to be successful Facebook marketing experts, and this is where the leverage started to be created.

I ended up working with and coaching some folks that were absolutely incredible at Facebook ads. You could tell that their mission was to be the BEST at Facebook ads. As for me, I accomplished my mission of helping business owners create a positive return on investment, and I was ready for my mission with Life on Fire to help others love what they do for work.

It was like being Mr. Miyagi and watching Daniel-san rise up and become an absolute master. So I'd like to introduce you to "Danielle-san" a.k.a. Valerie Shoopman. I also refer to her as "The Shoooop!"

I've worked with lots and lots of folks in Facebook advertising and marketing and haven't met anyone like Valerie. She is more than just a team member. She genuinely cares about my business and me as if her name was on all the checks too. She's reliable and does what she says all the time.

She is masterful with copy. She can take my outline for a webinar that I'm going to do and cook up all the ads and landing pages without having to tug at me for answers.

She's notorious for cutting lead costs in half and helping to create cash flow positive campaigns. She even finishes my sentences!

When you hire out your Facebook advertising, it gives you the leverage to work on other areas that may fall into your greatest skill set and, as a result, be the best use of your time. *which I did w Frances*

But it is definitely critical to be involved in the strategy. This should not be delegated. For me, I'm a strategy guy. You give me thirty minutes on the phone with an entrepreneur, and I'll narrow the niche, drill down to the target market, and frame out a marketing funnel that will totally change your business.

So when you combine strategy with exceptional Facebook ad management (Valerie), it's a killer combo.

Again, you HAVE to be involved even if you hire out your ads. Sales are the most important area of your business. Never, ever lose sight of that.

You will never be broke when you're good at sales.

The outcome of working with Valerie is that we've been able to break seven figures in 2014 alone. This makes for a seven-figure (per year) business in less than two years by leveraging the power of Facebook advertising and marketing.

You're probably not going to believe how easy it is to get to seven figures when you read the next chapter.

Wait a minute! Wait a minute! Don't let the money trick you!

What makes this business so successful is that I love what I do for work—creating success stories—each and every day. In addition, we're giving back an absolute ton of money to charity.

Now THAT is a Life on Fire!

And here's EXACTLY how we did it ...

Well, of course we are crystal clear on our "ideal" target market, and we have a narrow niche. We also spend our time wisely on activities that will get us where we want to go.

Here's where I would encourage you to invest the majority of your energy in your business:

One:

Over deliver to your customers and create success stories. This creates the "earned media" and a tribe of loyal advocates.

And yep, you guessed it—we ask for reviews, whether it's for our top-rated podcast on iTunes, *Life on Fire TV*, or our coaching programs.

Two:

Focus on profit-producing activities to bring in sales. We've tested just about every method of making sales in this industry: live events, sponsoring events, phone sales, Google ads, Twitter ads, YouTube ads, content marketing, blogging, video marketing, and Facebook advertising and marketing.

What's incredible about our sales growth is that more than 90 percent of our revenue comes from Facebook advertising. Even when we sell at a live event, we're able to bring on new clients because they will have first seen an ad on Facebook, then attended a webinar, and THEN decided to come to one of our events.

So when "Life on Fire.com" was launched, we put our focus on profit-producing activities. We didn't have any customers and we needed some—fast!

We knew from our collective experience that the best return on investment was to put all our focus on a simple Facebook marketing funnel: we would run an ad on Facebook to a webinar and then subsequently sell our products and services.

It's incredibly simple ...

Step 1: Identify your ideal target market.

Step 2: Create your lead magnet.

A resource that enables you to instantly set up a website that allows you to set one of these up with literally zero technical experience is www.leadpages.net. They have top-performing templates, and all you have to do is type in your copy and add a picture.

Step 3: Set up your Facebook ads.

Valerie is about to smash the ball out of the park in the following chapters about how to do this.

Step 4: Deliver a live webinar.

When you add value for your audience with a live webinar, your goal is to solve their problem and build a relationship.

Because you have a live audience, you have their undivided live attention, and you can encourage them to take the next step—whether that is a call with you or a purchase of one of your products or services.

Step 5: Over-deliver and create earned media.

Bring in those new customers, ask for reviews, and let them be your advocates that bring in new customers.

What's crazy to think about is that when we started running ads to a webinar with "Life on Fire," we didn't even have a website for www.LifeOnFire.com up yet.

Why?

Websites are not ATM machines that just spew money at you. They take time to build and grow so that they produce money. The sad thing is that it is extremely difficult to get organic traffic to your website to make sales. That is why we spend the majority of our time running Facebook ads to webinars where we make sales, over deliver, then rinse and repeat all the way to seven figures.

After doing hundreds and hundreds of coaching calls, I've found that one of the biggest distractions is working on your main website. It takes forever to write the copy and have it designed to your liking. The problem is that most of us entrepreneurs turn into perfectionists all of the sudden when it comes to building a website for ourselves.

The bottom line is that I knew that www.LifeOnFire.com would NOT pay the bills and would not create success stories. So we focused our energy on the simple Facebook webinar funnel.

Facebook Ads Allow You to Write Your Own Checks and Control Your Destiny:

Imagine what your life would look like if you could spend $1 in Facebook advertising and receive $2 back? Shoot, what if for every dollar you spent in Facebook ads you received $5 back? That's the reality of what happens when you become excellent at Facebook marketing. You're able to literally determine how fast you want to grow your revenues, how fast you want to build your e-mail list, and how fast you want to grow your authority.

When you, the reader, fully digest and comprehend Chapters 2–5, you will be in a position to run a webinar marketing funnel that can set your business and life on fire and give you everything you want. Wouldn't it be great to know that you could literally double your annual sales at any time that you want? It sounds crazy, but online sales is simple. It's all math.

What do I mean by that?

On one of our recent campaigns, we made $52,495 in total sales with just $7,472 in Facebook advertising spend. The best part is that it all happened within two weeks! That's quite a bit different from when I invested $30,000 in TV commercials to make $280.

Can you imagine what your life and business would be like that if you put $7,472 into Facebook ads to generate $52,495 of revenue? As I said before, when you nail Chapters 2–5 and understand your market, you'll be able to run Facebook ads and dramatically increase your revenues.

For "Life on Fire" this is exactly what we do: we help others achieve their goals. This is why we've been able to break seven figures within our second year in business. We simply run Facebook ads.

It's super important to know that running Facebook ads is the means to how you can grow revenues FAST, but the beautiful thing is that you can at the same time target truly "ideal" customers with whom you love to work.

When revenue comes in and you have excess, you can choose to give back (to charity) and add purpose to your business.

When you run Facebook ads, you build your brand at breakneck speeds. People always say to me, "Nick, I see you everywhere!" That's because they log into Facebook multiple times per day and BOOM! There I am again and again. When they think of Facebook marketing, they think of me.

It's all about increasing your mindshare in your ideal target market.

The best part is that you don't have to invest $30,000 like I did with Plummeting Profits. You can start with $5 per day and build yourself up until you're in a position to bring on a "Danielle-san" like Valerie to run it for you. If there was a faster or more efficient way to build a business, trust me—I would do it.

That's why I'm so fired up for you to dive into the next chapter with Valerie.

I've spent the first six chapters pages prepping you, and now Valerie is going to drive home the step-by-step process on how YOU can make Facebook marketing profitable in YOUR business.

You don't want to miss a single page. Take a second to commit to yourself and decide that you ARE going to set your business and life on fire.

Life's too short not to!

PART 2

Facebook Ads Step by Step

Hey! Valerie here and I hope you enjoyed what Nick laid out for you in the first half of the book! If you read through his strategies and thoroughly embraced the stories and marketing strategies in those chapters, then you'll be ready to rock with this second half of the book!

Whether you're brand new to Facebook ads or you're an experienced marketer, you'll get great value from the way I've laid this section of the book out in an easy-to-understand, step-by-step approach with supporting screenshots, videos, and downloadables.

Nick has already laid the foundation in the previous chapters with the mindset, strategies, and what's possible to achieve with Facebook ads. Now I'm going to teach you exactly how to get it done!

You'll learn step-by-step how to create Facebook ad campaigns that perform over and over again to drive targeted leads and loyal customers to your business so that YOU can live a "Life on Fire"!

Sound good?

Great! Let's dive in!

Chapter 7

Great Facebook Ad Strategies Start with the End in Mind

Nick Unsworth and Valerie Shoopman

-7-

Great Facebook Ad Strategies Start with the End In Mind

Just like Stephen Covey states in *The 7 Habits of Highly Effective People*, you need to start with the end goal in mind.

What are you trying to achieve with your Facebook ad campaign?

You need to have one clearly defined goal with results that are trackable. This goal will be your guiding light throughout the campaign and will enable you to measure the true success of your campaign.

Failure to define your goal and share it with your team will set your Facebook ad campaign up for failure. I know you don't want that!

So here are a few examples of the types of goals you might have for your Facebook ad campaigns. Remember, one measurable goal per campaign is ideal. This is not to say you won't hit other objectives, such as page likes, while you're building your list, but that is what I call gravy, and it is not where your focus should be as you set up and monitor the campaign.

You might run a **Like campaign** to increase your Facebook business page likes (number of fans), reach (who is seeing your brand and posts), and for social proof (your online authority).

Engagement campaigns allow you to promote specific page posts to reach more of your targeted audience and amplify your organic engagement strategies where you are getting more people to like, comment on, and share your content.

One of my all-time favorite goals is the **Lead-Generating campaign** to build your e-mail list. There's no better way to quickly build a very targeted list than with Facebook ads. You own your e-mail list and can take it with you from platform to platform. I highly encourage everyone to work on building their e-mail list as it's the backbone of any business.

Note: Facebook fans are not part of your list. You must work to encourage them to join your list through what we call lead magnets. Nick covered lead magnets in earlier chapters of the book, remember? He mentioned things like free downloads, free one-page reports, video training series, and **webinars** as good lead magnets.

You can run **Contest/Referral campaigns** as Nick talked about earlier in the book to build your list and create a buzz around your brand and products or services. The Referral campaign in particular is a great way to utilize Facebook ads for "earned media" or word-of-mouth advertising.

Retargeting campaigns allow you to reengage your list, buyers, and website visitors to help keep you top of mind, and to let them know what's happening in your world, such as a big event, promotion, or even celebrations of success. Remember, Facebook (and social media in general) is all about relationships and connecting with others. You want to build a deep relationship with your target audience.

You can also run **Sales Funnel campaigns** to drive targeted clients and potential clients to your offers. Generally speaking though, this method does not work as well as others because people aren't in a "buying" mindset when they are on Facebook. They're on Facebook to interact with their family and friends. However, people usually can't resist freebies and special discounts for products and services that they're interested in.

The key point here is "products and services that they're interested in." That means you need to be very good at targeting prospects with these types of offers. Most of the time, I prefer to give something of value first and then continue to build the relationship with them before mentioning the offer, especially if it is a high-end offer. Very, very rarely do high-end offers convert directly from an ad on Facebook.

If the budget is there, I like to run multiple campaigns all at one time. For example, I might run a Like campaign, an Engagement campaign, and a Lead-Generating campaign all at the same time.

Using those three campaigns in conjunction with each other, you can:

- First, bring in new, targeted potential clients as fans on your page
- Then encourage them and your other fans to like, comment on, and share your content (which can have a viral effect)
- Finally, give them something of such great value that they're willing to give you their name and e-mail address so that you can continue to follow up with them and build a relationship while helping them realize how your products and services can solve their problems

With each of these campaigns, there is a clearly defined, measurable goal. You can tell the total number of actions that happened and at what cost.

- Page likes
- Post engagement
- Opt-ins to your e-mail list

The kinds of campaign goals you have depend upon your business goals and budget.

You don't have to have a bunch of page likes to be successful if social proof isn't necessary for your industry. But if you're in an industry where social proof is a huge indicator of online authority and success, then you'd better run a Like campaign either first or in conjunction with another campaign.

If you don't have much ad spend budget but you have a solid offer and lead magnet, then I'd definitely go for the Lead-Generating campaign. Build your e-mail list and make your offer.

Say you don't have a lead magnet or offer yet, but you want to build up community. Then I'd go for an Engagement campaign so that you can build your brand, get your name out there, amplify your reach, and let people engage with you and your content. You can also ask questions to find out what their greatest challenges and frustrations are and then provide them with the exact solution to their problems. Genius way to go about product development, don't you think?!

What's Possible with the Different Campaign Objectives?

Currently you can get targeted page likes, and I mean very, very targeted (as in your ideal client) page likes for an average of 20 cents per page like in most niches. You used to be able to get that down under 10 cents per page like, but those days are mostly long gone unless you go for untargeted page likes which I would never recommend.

Like Campaign

I routinely get page post engagements in the range of 10–15 cents per engagement with click-through rates of 10 percent or more.

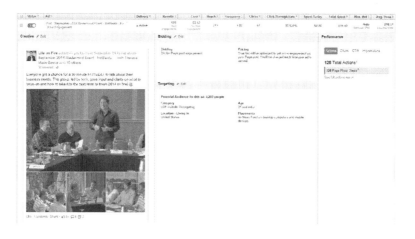

Page Post Engagement Campaign

I absolutely love getting targeted leads for less than $2 per opt-in! I consider those fantastic results. In most niches, a more reasonable expectation would be an average of $3–5 per opt-in, depending on the targeting and the offer.

Opt-in Lead Generation Campaign

Every once in a while it makes sense to do a direct sales campaign with Facebook ads. Key considerations include the following: Are you at least breaking even with your ad spend? Or are you using it as a loss leader, knowing that you have a way to upsell them into other products or services?

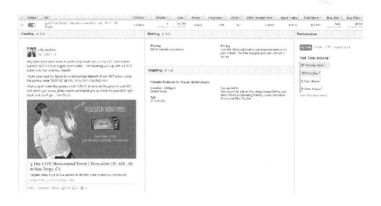

Direct Sales Funnel Campaign

Chapter 7 Recap:

- Start your Facebook ad campaign with the end goal in mind.
- Set one measurable goal per campaign.
- Like campaigns are good for social proof.
- Engagement campaigns can help amplify your message.
- Lead-Generation campaigns work the best on Facebook. A webinar funnel with a Facebook ad to an optin for a webinar is my all-time favorite lead-generation tool.
- Sales Funnel campaigns (with direct sales offers) are the most difficult to make work with Facebook ads because people are not in a "buying" mindset when they're on Facebook, scrolling through their newsfeed.

Chapter 7 Resources:

- Book – *The 7 Habits of Highly Effective People* – Stephen Covey
- Video – *Like Campaign*

http://www.thebookonfbmarketing.com/resources

Chapter 8

Facebook Ad Campaign Success – It's All in the Flow

Nick Unsworth and Valerie Shoopman

-8-

Facebook Ad Campaign Success – It's All in the Flow

You might be wondering what I mean by "It's All in the Flow."

"It's all in the flow" refers to the idea that the funnel needs to flow seamlessly from ad to landing page to thank-you page to e-mail follow-up to the offer page. The branding—including the images, colors, fonts, and languaging—needs to be congruent across all points of the funnel, and it needs to speak to your ideal target audience.

When your funnel seamlessly flows from the ad to the landing page to the thank-you page to the e-mail follow-up to the offer, the potential client feels comfortable and safe. You're answering their exact questions and objections while offering them real solutions, thus bringing them further along in the "like, know, and trust" cycle.

All the components in the funnel either work together to build trust, increase conversions, and lower acquisition costs, or they work against each other, causing objections and mistrust. As soon as the objections and mistrust start, you lose them—wherever that may be in the funnel. Then, your conversions go down, and your costs go up.

I like to start with the offer and then work backwards toward the Facebook ad from there.

So, for example, when starting with the offer, I make sure the price point or goal justifies the ad costs. Then I take a look at whom the offer is targeting and what problem it is solving. I'll also take a look at the images and see if any of them, or a portion of them, can be used on the landing page, thank-you page, and in the ad.

Note that in some funnels, like a webinar funnel, the offer won't come until later, at the end of the webinar. But I still like to build the offer page out first so that it will all flow and make sense as someone is coming step-by-step through the funnel.

Then I use the images, headlines, and copy that make sense from the offer page on the landing page. Think of the landing page as a shorter version of the offer page with only one, very clear call to action, such as "Enter your name and e-mail address to get xyz so that your business and life will be transformed." *you*

+ your work will be remembered.

Leadpages is a very easy-to-use, online software platform that allows you to build landing pages and thank-you pages quickly from preformatted templates. You can also adjust the style settings so that the colors and fonts match your branding. They are adding more and more templates and features all the time to make this process as quick, easy, and flexible as possible. The ability to test different things and get your funnel up and running quickly is invaluable.

Once your landing page is built, you need to create your thank-you page. Again, use the same style and branding to make it congruent as your potential client is working their way through your funnel. The thank-you page is one of the most underutilized pages in most funnels. Use it not only to thank them for taking action, but to further the relationship with them right then and there, guiding them to what to do next and what to expect.

Now that we have the landing page and thank-you page built, we can create the Facebook ad. Again, we take the headlines and copy that make sense from the offer page and landing page along with any images, and we keep the colors and fonts the same or as similar as possible. Also, make sure the ad speaks directly to your target audience from the WIIFM (What's In It For Me) frame of mind Nick talked about in earlier chapters.

The biggest difference between creating the ad and the landing page is you're going to make it personal. Very personal. Remember, people are on Facebook to interact with their family and friends, not to search for products and services. So the image needs to preferably be a lifestyle photo of you smiling, one that conveys an emotional response, or a photo that stands out in the newsfeed so much that people have to click on it just to see what's going on.

Remember, you'll be targeting your ads very narrowly, so you'll want as many people to click on your ad as possible because each one of them will be your ideal client if you've narrowed your niche and done your homework researching where those ideal clients hang out on Facebook.

Experiment with different accent colors, headlines, and calls to action in the photo to see what gets the best results. Clicks and conversions dictate what's working the best, not what you or your friends think will work the best. Sometimes, it's hard to put our ego aside and take a look at the hard, cold facts of the number of clicks and the cost per conversion. This is where a clearly defined campaign goal, along with conversion tracking, will help you determine what's working and what's not working.

Make sure the copy in your ad is personal too. Write the copy just like you were posting on your personal timeline for your best friend to read—except your best friend is your ideal client, and you're solving one of their biggest problems in their life or business at the moment.

Then you can write your follow-up e-mails to go in your autoresponder that continue to deepen the relationship and bring your ideal prospect along the "like, know, and trust" cycle based on how they respond to certain offers and calls to action.

One of the best things you can do is build out your funnel and then go through it a couple times (see if someone else can go through it for you as well) to catch any mishaps, technical glitches, and conflicting information. Make sure you test your funnel both on a desktop and mobile device so that you have that experience and can control the placement of the ad if necessary.

Chapter 8 Recap:

- Start with the offer and work backwards from there to the Facebook ad.
- The landing page should line up with the offer and your ideal target audience.
- Compare the Facebook ad to the landing page.
- There should be consistency and congruency between all parts of the funnel.
- The ad targeting and languaging should reach the right audience with the proper message.
- Your copy should be written from the WIIFM (What's In It For Me) perspective of your ideal client.
- Going forward from the Facebook ad clear through to the end of the funnel, everything should work. Every piece of the funnel should look and feel congruent. There should be no issues if you were seeing the funnel for the first time.

Chapter 8 Resources:

- Get Leadpages to build out your funnel
  http://smarturl.it/GetLeadPages
- Video – *How to Use Leadpages*

http://www.thebookonfbmarketing.com/resources

Nick Unsworth and Valerie Shoopman

Chapter 9

Setting Up the Structure of Your Facebook Ad Campaigns

Nick Unsworth and Valerie Shoopman

-9-

Setting Up the Structure of Your Facebook Ad Campaigns

To begin to use the Facebook advertising platform, you'll need a personal profile set up on Facebook. It's free and very easy to set up. Hopefully, you already have that done!

You'll also need to set up a Facebook business page because you can't advertise to your personal profile. Think of your Facebook business page as your mini website.

If you're just starting out, then I'd highly suggest you actually skip the website for now, build your Facebook business page (which is quick and easy), and then put all your focus on getting clients. As you start to work with clients, you'll figure out their objections, what packages you should provide, and the other things you'll need to know to build out your website right the first time.

Now, back to the Facebook business page! It's a necessity to have before you can begin to advertise on Facebook. It's also a way for people to find you, both inside Facebook and in online search engines such as Google or Bing.

Yep, that's right! If you set your Facebook business page up correctly, you'll not only be able to advertise in Facebook, but you'll also be able to optimize it to show up in the search engines for specific keywords and locations.

Here are a few key things to keep in mind when setting up your business page:

People like to relate to people, not brands, so if you don't have a brand yet, consider using just your name and brand yourself. If you do have a brand, consider having a person be the face of that brand and use their photo as the profile pic for the page.

Make sure you fill out all the information in the "About" section, including keywords for your specific products and services, but don't stuff in keywords just to get them in there. Make sure the text still flows naturally as you're reading it.

You'll also want to include your exact location if you have one so that people will be able to leave you reviews and so that you can benefit from that "earned media" Nick talked about in the beginning.

You can find a complete walk-through of how to set up your Facebook business page at thebookonfbmarketing.com/resources. Once you have your business page set up, then run it through the free Likealyzer app at http://likealyzer.com/ to get a free review of your page. It will even provide exact steps you can take to improve the effectiveness and ranking of your page.

Once your business page is set up and published, you'll want to set up your Facebook ad account, which is fairly straightforward. You'll need to have your credit card handy and then go to

https://www.facebook.com/ads/manage/billing.php and select "Payment Methods" from the left-hand text menu. Enter your Facebook password, then enter your payment information, and you're good to go.

Now you're ready to set up your first ad campaign! Click on "Campaigns" from the left-hand text menu or go to

https://www.facebook.com/ads/manage.

Click on the green "Create Ad" button in the top right-hand corner or go to https://www.facebook.com/ads/create/ to begin creating your ad.

Remember in the previous chapter where I talked about the goal of your Facebook ad campaign? This is where you're going to set up your predefined goal for this ad campaign.

You can choose to send people to your website, promote conversions on your website, boost your post, promote your page, get installs of your app, increase engagement in your app, raise attendance at your event, get people to claim your offer, or get video views.

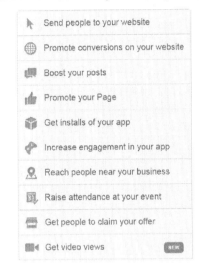

Advertise on Facebook   Help: Choosing an Objective

What kind of results do you want for your ads?

- Send people to your website
- Promote conversions on your website
- Boost your posts
- Promote your Page
- Get installs of your app
- Increase engagement in your app
- Reach people near your business
- Raise attendance at your event
- Get people to claim your offer
- Get video views

This sounds like a lot, doesn't it? That's why you need to have a clearly defined, measurable goal before you start your campaign!

I tend to use the "promote conversions on your website," the "boost your post," and the "promote your page" options the most.

"Promote conversions on your website" enables you to do just that. You can set up a conversion tracking code and track the number of conversions, such as opt-ins, that occur from a Facebook ad. Then you'll also be able to track the cost of those conversions.

"Boost your post" enables you to run ads to specific posts on your page and control who sees the ads. This is different from the "boost post" you see on your actual page. You have much more control when you use this function from within the Ads Manager Dashboard. The main reason to use this is to get more engagement and reach on a particular post so that more people will see it and then like, share, and comment on the post.

"Promote your page" is a specific campaign to get page likes to your Facebook business page. You want to do this for a few reasons, including social proof (as we've talked about before), and also because usually (if you have targeted fans) the conversions will be higher and the costs lower when advertising to fans of your page versus cold Facebook traffic from other pages.

Once you set your goal for the campaign, it's time to understand a bit about the campaign structure.

In the hierarchy of Facebook campaigns, you have **campaigns** (which can have only one goal per campaign) on the top level, then your **ad sets** on the middle level (where you can control things like daily ad spend and start and stop times of the ads), and finally the **ads** themselves (where you set up the creative aspects of the ad and the targeting).

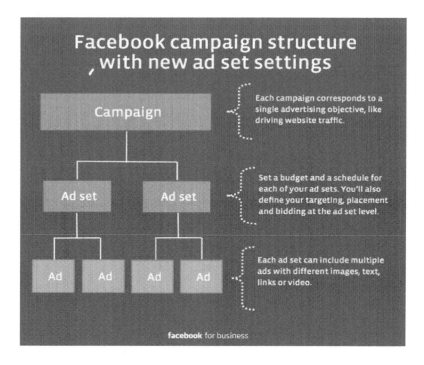

Facebook makes it easy to run multiple ad sets per campaign, and they also make it easy to run multiple ads per ad set. However, I'd suggest that you don't run multiple ads per ad set because you are giving complete control to Facebook over how and when those ads within the ad set are shown. This makes it difficult to split test variables, such as demographics and targeting, because you have no control over what percentage of time each ad is being shown to what group.

Here's a little trick I learned from my Google Adwords days of being an affiliate marketer!

I set it up so that there is only one ad per ad set so that I have complete control and can do an effective split test on what's working and what's not working. This is what allows you to scale up what's working and pause out what's not working so that you get the best conversions at the lowest cost.

So say, for example, you have a webinar you're promoting for your new product. You can set up one campaign for "promote conversions on your website," then set up an ad set with one ad that targets just your fan page. Then set up another ad set with one ad that targets just one of your competitors' fan pages.

You can set up as many of these separate ad sets with one ad each as makes sense for your targeting and budget. You'll be able to quickly and clearly see which one is converting and at what cost. Then you can effectively pause the ones that aren't working and increase the budget on the ones that are.

When you are creating Facebook ads, there are two tools that Facebook provides for you. The first is the Ads Manager Dashboard, which is the most popular (especially with beginners) because it's the easiest to use.

Ads Manager Dashboard

However, that ease of use comes with a price: you don't have as many options or as much control as you do with the other tool Facebook provides—The Power Editor.

The Power Editor is a bit clunky on the user-interface side of things (although it's gotten much better in the past few months!), but it gives you complete control with the maximum number of options for creating and implementing your ads.

Power Editor

The other thing we need to talk about, regardless of whether you use the Ads Manager Dashboard or the Power Editor, is bidding strategies.

I personally like to use optimized CPM (or oCPM), which is optimized cost per impression where it's done for 1,000 impressions at a time. This may sound complicated, but it's not really.

Basically, you are paying so much for every 1,000 people that see your ad. If you're doing optimized CPM, then you can choose how you want Facebook to optimize how your ad is shown. Facebook can show your ad to people who have historically taken a specific action within your target audience.

If your ad is targeted and congruent, then people will click on it and take the action you want them to take. That way you're not paying for clicks when people aren't specifically interested in what's on the other side of the click or when they are just click happy.

That being said, if you're not sure about your targeting or how your audience might react to your ad, or if time is very short, then you might want to do CPC or cost per click. That way you are paying for every click that occurs, so you can more readily see what is appealing to people and what's not at a quicker rate.

As far as bidding, I always go higher than the highest range suggested by Facebook. I've never once paid even close to that, and it always ensures my ad is shown and usually in a top spot.

Use your reports and Ad Campaign Dashboard to monitor your ads so that your ad spend doesn't run away on you. Remember, you always have control over the daily ad spend and the ability to stop your ads at any time.

Of course, you should always, always, test, test, test to see what works best for your particular niche and for each campaign within your niche.

Chapter 9 Recap:

- You need to set up and optimize a Facebook business page before you can run ads.
- You need to set up your Facebook ad account.
- Choose your campaign goal (end result).
- Know the Facebook ad hierarchy: campaigns, ad sets, ads.
- Use the one ad per ad set strategy to get the maximum results for the lowest cost.
- Let Facebook optimize your bidding as much as possible.

Chapter 9 Resources:

- Website / App – Likealyzer to analyze your Facebook business page – http://likealyzer.com/
- Facebook Ad Manager – https://www.facebook.com/ads/manage

Chapter 10

Nailing the Facebook Ad Creatives

-10-

Nailing the Facebook Ad Creatives

Before you actually create your first ad, you need to have all the creatives laid out and ready to plug into the appropriate spots. This will make it so much easier and quicker to get the actual ad created and ready for Facebook to approve.

The image is the most important thing for your ad!

We live in a more visual time where people read less and look more at images for what they want to know.

Don't forget—people are on Facebook to interact with their friends and family, so you'll definitely want a personal image, preferably one of you smiling in a lifestyle-type photo. Pick one that stands out with colors or objects or because of a difference in the way the photo was taken.

These are all good ways to grab attention. Remember how Nick talked about the billboard image and what you see driving by at 70 mph? That's what you want for the newsfeed and right-side images. You're trying to grab their attention first and then convey an emotional response—all with one image if possible.

You can also add text, such as short headlines or a call to action on the photo. Be sure you don't go over the 20 percent text rule Facebook has in place for images used in ads though.

You can use Facebook's grid tool at

https://www.facebook.com/help/468870969814641 to see if your text is under the 20 percent limitation. If you use Photoshop, you can also turn on your grid to view it and check your image to make sure the text is not taking up more than 20 percent of the image.

You'll want to test several different images for each campaign if possible. The worst thing you can do is try only one image and then say the campaign didn't work!

Always let the clicks and conversions decide which image is a winner. Don't let your ego get in the way. Just because it's your favorite image doesn't mean it's going to be the image that converts the best!

For the technical details, make sure your photo is 1,200 pixels wide by 628 pixels tall. That size will be the best image resolution across all ad formats.

If you have Photoshop and know how to use it, that's the best tool for creating your images. However, it has a steep cost and learning curve.

The good news is there are two great free programs out there that you can use and get just the same if not better results!

Gimp is a great Photoshop alternative that's free! You can download it at http://www.gimp.org/.

Canva is an online image tool that is super easy to use. You just select what type of image you want to create, and then you can use the predefined templates to pop in your image and text. You can access Canva for free at https://www.canva.com/.

The Headline

Now you need to write an attention-grabbing headline to go with your awesome image!

Use your headlines to grab people's attention and alert them as to why they should pay attention to what you are saying in that short snippet of time you have as your ad flies by in their Facebook newsfeed. Headlines should complement your image you have selected, and both should ideally be able to stand on their own if necessary without any additional copy.

Don't forget to make sure the ad is congruent with the landing page like we talked about earlier. You want your potential client to feel like they've taken another natural step along the path to learning more about how to solve their problem. You don't want them to feel uncomfortable or like they've arrived on a page that has nothing to do with what the ad suggested.

Questions work well in headlines, in addition to direct calls to action that guide the reader to take the desired action. Numbers tend to stand out from the other text if you can work them in. Capitalize each word in the headline to help draw attention too. Every little bit helps when constructing a headline!

Also, keep in mind the phrase "so that"—so that you'll make more money, so that you'll have more time, so that you'll have more freedom, so that you'll get more clients, etc. Sometimes you can work it into the headline, but you need to be sure to work it into the copy supporting the headline! Always go back to the WIIFM (What's In It For Me) mindset.

Here are a few headline examples to learn from and get your creative juices flowing:

CLICK HERE to Learn My Simple Method for Holding Consultations

Need Help Recruiting?

How One Small Switch Can Increase Your Conversion Rates By 75%

Do You Struggle Selling From Teleseminars and Webinars Online?

FREE Facebook Photo Templates

[FREE WEBINAR] How To Build A 6-Figure Social Media Management Company

[LIVE EVENT] How To Grow Your 6-Figure Business Into A 7-Figure Business

5 Brutally Honest Dating Rules To Live By

Boost Your Meditation Results

FREE EVENT | Life On Fire Virtual Summit 2014

Copy That Connects

Make sure you keep the copy (what's in the post section of the ad) personal! One of the biggest mistakes I see people make with Facebook ads is not keeping the copy personal.

Remember, people get on Facebook to interact with their friends and family. That is where their mindset is and what they are expecting, so you need to follow along that path of friendliness to connect and interact with them.

Also, make sure you make it congruent with what's on your landing page, and write it from the WIIFM (What's In It For Me) perspective.

Here are a couple examples that would go in the post copy section of your Facebook ads:

1st Example:

Hey there! Did you know I'm running a free training webinar all about how to use Twitter to attract more ideal customers? In this LIVE training, you will learn:

1. A Quick and Easy Way to Drive Targeted Traffic to Your Website and Grow Your E-mail List.

2. The Proven Twitter Marketing Plan to Sell Your Products, Programs, and Services.

3. The Underground Method to Find Customers Now on Twitter.

Click the link below to join me on this FREE Webinar where I'll show you how to use Twitter to Attract More Customers! Can't wait to share all the deets with you! :)

2nd Example:

I'm super fired up to bring you this virtual summit with 24 of the most sought after speakers I handpicked for this special event! They'll be sharing their personal success strategies based around purpose, mindset, marketing, and networking. Our mission is to help you build your business and live a life on fire AND support Pencils of Promise to build a school in Guatemala. Hop on board this puppy to catch the Virtual Success Train and start living a Life On Fire! :)

Calls to Action

It sounds a bit silly in this day and age, but people still need to be told what to do. Yep, you need to tell them to click the image below to sign up, or click here to register for the FREE webinar!

The good thing is when you put those calls to action in the text, the percentage rate of people taking that action is much higher!

Putting It All Together

To make it easier, I create the headline, copy, and call to action all in a text file and save it so that it's easy to copy and paste to create new ads and in case something happens and I lose my work. That way, I don't have to think of the creative all over again. Yes, Facebook does have glitches every once in a while, so better to be safe than sorry!

Chapter 10 Recap:

- Use personal, lifestyle images of you smiling with colors that pop in a 1,200 x 628 format.
- Don't use more than 20 percent text on the image.
- Use attention-grabbing headlines that make the reader want to click and find out more.
- Include copy that's personal and connects with people as if they're your friends.
- Include calls to action to tell people exactly what you want them to do.

Chapter 10 Resources:

- Gimp – a free Photoshop-like photo editing program at http://www.gimp.org/
- Canva – a free, template-based photo editing tool at https://www.canva.com/
- Video – *How to Use Photoshop to Create Facebook Ad Images*
- Video – *Ads Manager Dashboard*
- Video – *Power Editor 101*

http://www.thebookonfbmarketing.com/resources

Chapter 11

Using Facebook Ad Targeting to Market Only to Your Ideal Clients

Nick Unsworth and Valerie Shoopman

-11-

Using Facebook Ad Targeting to Market Only to Your Ideal Clients

We've talked quite a bit about ideal clients and the need to narrow the focus of your campaign down to one ideal target audience. This still trips a lot of people up. They don't want to feel like they are losing out on business, so they want to market to everyone, or they genuinely feel they can help a wider scope of clients.

Here's the deal. When you try to help everyone, you end up helping no one because no one feels you're really speaking to them. You're not reaching them on an emotional level because you don't have that very specific avatar (or best friend) that you can speak directly to their needs, wants, and desires.

I think everyone goes through this at one point or another in their business. When you're mired in the depths of trying to please everyone, it's hard to see that's what you're doing and that there's an easier (and more effective!) way of going about it.

I'll use myself as an example to drive home the point of how crucial it is to narrowly define your niche and target audience.

When I first met Nick, I was a "social media manager" with a huge technology background, which meant I could do a lot of things. I could work in Facebook, Twitter, YouTube, and LinkedIn. I could work on setting up your autoresponder. I could set up a sales page. I could work in the backend of nearly any software program.

Every day I was doing something different, which was good because it kept me from getting bored, but not so good if you wanted to get really deep into something or become a true expert at it.

Nick told me I needed to narrow my niche and become known for something. I told him I was good at lots of things, and that kept it interesting. He said I would always struggle until I narrowed my niche and that I needed to pick something, anything, just pick one thing to be known for. We went back and forth like this for a while. I mean, I really dug in my heels about this. I'd always known how to do a lot of things, and I didn't want to get stuck doing just one single thing.

Then I had the idea to ask a couple friends for feedback. I asked them, when they thought of my name, what did they think of business-wise about me. They both told me that they weren't quite sure what I did. They knew I did something online with computers, and one friend said she knew I had a business name, but she could never remember it—"Social Media" something or another.

The lightning bolt had finally struck! Even my closest friends didn't know exactly what I did or what the name of my business was. How could I expect anyone else (much less a potential client) to know what I did or remember the name of my business?

So, I decided to heed Nick's advice and pick something to be known for. Facebook was the social media platform I liked the best, it was popular, and it had an advertising platform that I thought was easy and others thought was hard. So, bam! In a split second, I decided I would become a Facebook marketing expert who specialized in Facebook ads.

The transformation that happened once I made this transition was astounding!

I now could focus solely on Facebook without having to worry about keeping up on all the other platforms. I was working in Facebook day in and day out, not jumping from thing to thing, project to project, platform to platform. This allowed me to go really deep into Facebook and become a true expert on Facebook marketing and, in particular, Facebook ads.

The outside world began to see me in a different light too. I was beginning to be called The Facebook Ad Queen, The

No-Fluff Facebook Ad Queen, The Go-To Woman for Facebook, etc. In fact, now when people heard my name, they almost immediately thought "Facebook marketing" and "Facebook ads."

What a drastic shift!

People now associated me with something specific (Facebook marketing and ads) that I was really good at. This meant now it was super easy for them to remember me, what I did, and more importantly recommend me and my services to their friends and business associates when the topic of Facebook marketing and running Facebook ads came up.

Needless to say, word-of-mouth referral marketing went through the roof after this. However, not all the referrals coming to me were what I considered ideal clients.

So I started focusing on using languaging that talked about how I liked to work with online business coaches that I could help effectively reach even more entrepreneurs with their products and services. I absolutely love the idea and the community around entrepreneurs, helping other entrepreneurs and working together to make a true difference in each other's lives, which will have a ripple effect felt around the world.

This all brings me to the target market or your ideal audience with Facebook ads. If I were running ads for my business right now, I'd be focusing on online business coaches whose focus was helping other entrepreneurs.

The following are a few ways I can go about finding them and where exactly they hang out on Facebook.

Google Search

Graph Search

Audience Insights

Custom Audiences

A lot of people don't actually think about the first way. You can switch platforms and do a **Google search** for keywords related to your ideal client. In my case, that might be "top business coaches," "top business coaching programs," "online business coaches," and "mentor to online business coaches." Also, don't forget to add "Facebook" to the search string to find their Facebook pages easily, or to look at the fantastic related searches Google puts at the bottom of page one of every search you do. In my case, look at the additional research paths I can take:

business mentor ***coaching llc***

small business online ***coach***

business ***train*** online ***booking***

mentors and business coaches ***international***

business ***coaching and mentoring tips***

*business **coaching and mentoring courses***

*mentor **coach job description***

*mentor **coach reviews***

When you research this way, I suggest you open each one in a new tab on your browser and also keep a notepad handy to jot down the myriad of ideas that will pop into your head as you go deeper and deeper into this ideal client.

Just as Amazon offers related products, you need to think like that here too. So always be thinking, "If my ideal client likes this, then they'll also probably like that because they're related or needed together so that ..." (fill in the blank, "are more efficient," "save time," "save money," etc.).

Next, I like to go to Facebook and do what is called a **graph search**. It sounds complicated, but it's a lot like a Google search; you simply do it within Facebook and use certain phrases to get the info you need instead of focusing so much on keywords.

You type these phrases in at the top of Facebook where it says "Search for people, places, and things." The object is to find pages with which your ideal target audience engages and likes. Here are a few examples of the types of phrases you can type into the Facebook graph search:

Groups of people who like PAGE NAME

Groups of people who like PAGE NAME and PAGE NAME

Favorite interests of people who like PAGE NAME

Employers liked by people who like PAGE NAME

Pages liked by people who like PAGE NAME

Pages liked by GENDER who like PAGE NAME

People who live in (city or state) and like PAGE NAME

Favorite interests of people who like PAGE NAME and PAGE NAME

Pages liked by INTEREST

Groups of people who are interested in INTEREST

Groups of people who like TOPIC and like PAGE NAME

People who like PAGE NAME/TOPIC and checked in at PLACE

TYPE OF BUSINESS in LOCATION visited by people who like PAGE NAME

Pages liked by GENDER who like PAGE NAME

Pages liked by people over the age of NUMBER who like PAGE NAME

Games played by fans of PAGE NAME

Again, have your notepad handy to make note of the particular pages and interests that come up. Just because there is a Facebook page doesn't mean they'll necessarily come up in the interest section of Facebook ads. There seems to be no rhyme or reason to this, so don't get frustrated; just make notes and take the ones available to you. I like to write them all down and then put a checkmark by the ones that are in the interest section of Facebook ads. Then I create a notepad file from those that I can easily reference and copy/paste for later.

To stick with my example above of business coaches, I might type in "Pages liked by people who like Nick Unsworth" or "Employers liked by people who like Life on Fire".

Audience Insights is a relatively new tool Facebook has provided to make it possible to research different demographics, interests, and trends of people on Facebook. You can find audience insights on the left-hand text menu from the Ads Manager Dashboard or at

https://www.facebook.com/ads/audience_insights.

Use this tool to research and find out more about different audiences, whether that is across all of Facebook, a particular interest, your Facebook business page, your competitor's page, or a custom audience you've built.

I love to use it to find what type of demographics a particular page or interest has as well as what other pages they like (get that notepad back out and make a note of these!), and one of the most important tabs I look at is the activity tab. I can see how much engagement is going on at a glance and how often they click on ads—über important if you're going to advertise to that group!

You could literally spend hours in the Audience Insights gathering data. To make this process easier and quicker for you, I've created a video where I walk you through the areas I've found to be the most beneficial. You can access it at http://www.thebookonfbmarketing.com/resources.

Custom Audiences is yet another way Facebook provides to be able to reach your ideal target market. It's one of my favorite (and most profitable!) ways to advertise on Facebook.

You have to build your custom audiences one at time through the audiences link at https://www.facebook.com/ads/manage/audiences.php. But the good news is once they're built, they are there for you to use in any ad at any time. You can also easily update the audiences.

To break it down a bit more for you...

There are several types of custom audiences to choose from. I find these three to be of the most value for the majority of my clients:

Data File Custom Audience

179

Website Custom Audience

Lookalike Custom Audience

The "Data File Custom Audience" allows you to upload data files, such as your e-mail list, to Facebook. You might wonder why in the world you'd want to do that when you already have their e-mail address. Well, when people see you in their e-mail and on Facebook, you automatically rise in importance to them on their radar screen. You stay top of mind and help convince them to take the time and effort to open your e-mail or find out more about your new program or service.

These are your warmest leads that will convert the best at the lowest cost—the low-hanging fruit, if you will. Don't make the mistake of leaving it untapped!

The "Website Custom Audience" is just like it sounds. It's an audience built from visitors to your website. You can set specific time periods and specific URLs if you choose, or you can keep it simple and just have it collect everyone who has previously visited your website anytime within the last 180 (maximum number) days.

These are people who are farther along the "know, like, and trust" cycle because they've actively visited your website for one reason or another in the past. That means they've heard about you and your products and services at some point and made an effort to go find out more. While these leads aren't as warm as your e-mail list, they are still very interested in you and your services and convert quite nicely over to your list to be further nurtured so that you can build a deeper relationship with them.

The "Lookalike Custom Audience" is a great tool to use to expand your reach and have Facebook do all the heavy lifting for you. You can choose a list such as your e-mail list or your website custom audience for Facebook to do the heavy lifting and go find similar folks who are already on Facebook. You can also choose your Facebook business pages from which you can create similar lists.

The one thing I'll say about Lookalike Custom Audiences is that while they're great, quick tools for expanding reach, most of the time the audiences they generate are huge. For that reason, I like to do what I call layering—I'll use the Lookalike Custom Audience, but I'll also put in an interest like "Social Media Examiner," a job title like "Founder," or a behavior like "Small Business Owner".

So now that you've narrowed your niche, focused in on your ideal target audience, and have ways to research how to reach that target audience on Facebook, you need a strategy for grouping or layering your audiences and for deciding whom to reach out to first.

If we look at your target audience in terms of hot, warm, and cold audiences, most likely your hot audience will be your e-mail list you uploaded as a custom audience. If you've built a good relationship with your list, you can expect this audience to convert the best at the lowest cost for your products and services.

Your website custom audience may fall into your hot audience or your warm audience depending upon your niche and website traffic. I find this is usually the second-best converting audience.

Your own Facebook business page should be in your warm audience sector as these people have heard of you and, at the very least, liked your page.

I like to use these audiences to test images, headlines, and copy against each other to quickly see what's working the best.

If you layer up your lookalike audiences for these three audiences (e-mail list, website custom audience, Facebook fan page) as I explained above, those can fall into your warm audience as well.

Once I find out what ad creative is working best, then I expand to totally cold traffic (think competitors' pages, other interests, job titles, other lookalike audiences, etc.) that probably hasn't heard of the person, product, or service being advertised.

Usually, this traffic is going to convert the least at the highest cost. It will, however, give you a way to keep branding yourself, keep your name in front of new potential prospects, get them to like your page, and add them to your e-mail list to take the relationship a step further down the line.

When you advertise to hot, warm, and cold audiences at the same time, you can be assured of conversions right now at an overall lower cost. In addition, you'll be bringing new potential prospects into your funnel to be further nurtured and brought along the sales cycle.

Chapter 11 Recap:

- Narrow your niche and have only one ideal target audience per ad campaign.
- Use Google Search, Graph Search, and Audience Insights to research more about your ideal target audience and where they hang out at on Facebook.
- Use Custom Audiences to build super-targeted audiences that will absolutely love your products and services.
- Group your ideal target audience into hot, warm, and cold audiences to advertise to them at the right time with realistic expectations for each grouping's outcome.

Chapter 11 Resources:

- Video – *Audience Insights*
- Video – *Creating Custom Audiences*

http://www.thebookonfbmarketing.com/resources

Nick Unsworth and Valerie Shoopman

Chapter 12

Facebook Conversion Tracking Pixels – The Secret Sauce

Nick Unsworth and Valerie Shoopman

-12-

Facebook Conversion Tracking Pixels – The Secret Sauce

We've been talking about all the strategies and mechanics that go into making a good Facebook ad campaign.

Facebook conversion tracking pixels are the secret sauce that can help you take an ad campaign from failing to working—and by working, I mean turning ad dollars into profit! Even better, when everything else is aligned and in place, they can also allow you to take an ad campaign from just working to getting fantastic results, which includes increased conversions at a lower cost per conversion.

Think of Nick's example earlier where we took $7,472 worth of ad spend and turned it into $52,495 worth of sales through an optimized funnel and a Facebook ad campaign. I don't know about you, but I'll take those results all day long!

I remember the days (long ago!) before Facebook had conversion tracking pixels. Yikes! I cringe just thinking about it. I call that flying blind, which is something I try to completely avoid!

I came from the Google Adwords platform, which by that time was pretty well developed, so I had been patiently waiting as Facebook rolled out each new feature that simplified and enhanced the overall ad experience. They still have a ways to go, but they're making great progress!

So, back to the conversion tracking pixels ...

The pixels themselves aren't really complicated. You just need to make sure to create them before you start ads, remember to attach them to the ads you create, and then use the reports to see what's converting and what's not.

You can create the conversion tracking pixels from the Conversion Tracking text link on the left-side menu of the Ads Manager Dashboard or go straight to https://www.facebook.com/ads/manage/convtrack.

Click on the green "Create Pixel" button in the top right-hand corner and then select a category. This is when your goal or objective for the campaign comes in handy. Is your goal to get leads? Or maybe opt-ins for your webinar? (Advanced users can create multiple tracking pixels for each campaign.)

Once you select an appropriate category, give it a name you'll easily recognize, such as "September Webinar XYZ Registrations." Then click the create button.

Facebook pops up a nice, neat little snippet of code that you can then copy and paste in between the head tags on the appropriate page. The correct page for the conversion tracking is always the page that comes after your customers have taken the action (e.g., the thank-you page after they've entered in their name and e-mail address).

If you don't mess with any code on your website, then give this code to your web designer and tell them what page to put it on. If you don't have a web designer, then Lead Pages is a very simple alternative that makes it easy to paste the tracking code in the proper place.

Once you've created the code and placed it on the correct page, you can attach the conversion tracking code to each ad you create. (Note: only some campaign objectives allow conversion tracking pixels. I prefer the website clicks or website conversion tracking objectives in almost all cases.)

You need only one conversion tracking pixel per goal for all the ads you create. This seems to be an area that trips a lot of people up.

For example, if you created a conversion tracking pixel for your webinar opt-ins, then you would attach that same conversion tracking pixel to each ad you create (in the Ads Manager Dashboard or Power Editor) for your webinar registration campaign. Facebook will then show each ad with the appropriate number of conversions that took place originating from that particular ad.

You can see this in the Ads Manager Dashboard, but I think it's much easier to discern the information in the reporting feature of Facebook, provided you make some edits to the layout of the generic report form. You can access the reports from the Reports text link on the left-hand side of the Ads Manager Dashboard, or go to https://www.facebook.com/ads/manage/reporting.php. Once there, click on the "Edit Columns" button to adjust the columns to your own unique needs.

For a high-level overview, I like to set it to show the campaign, ad set, ad, spend, conversion action (e.g., registration), and the cost of the conversion action. This gives you a clear view of the ultimate goal you've set for the campaign and at what cost those conversions are happening. Then you can make good decisions about which ads to pause and which ads to scale up.

Make sure you save this report layout with the save button so that you can easily return to it without having to reset the columns each time. If you need to troubleshoot your campaigns further, you can edit the columns appropriately.

Chapter 12 Recap:

- Create conversion tracking pixels for each campaign goal before you start your ads.
- Place the conversion tracking pixels on the page after the required action is taken.
- Customize the reports to see what's working and what's not working so that you can make adjustments to maximize the effectiveness of your campaign ad spend.

Chapter 12 Resources:

- Video – *How to Create and Place Conversion Tracking Pixels*
- Video – *How to Setup, Customize and Interpret the Reports to See What's Working and What's Not*

http://www.thebookonfbmarketing.com/resources

Chapter 13

Pulling It All Together for Successful Facebook Ad Campaigns in 6 Easy Steps

Nick Unsworth and Valerie Shoopman

-13-

Pulling It All Together for Successful Facebook Ad Campaigns in 6 Easy Steps

1. Know your target audience: demographics, likes, dislikes, challenges and frustrations, successes, languaging. Really get into their mind and see things from their vantage point, and then solve their problem.

2. Have an offer (product or service) that solves their biggest challenge or frustration at a price point that will sell and have enough ROI to run ads.

3. Create a landing page that is congruent with your offer and gives one clear call to action.

4. Create conversion tracking pixels to track your campaign goals

5. Create multiple ads with multiple images, headlines, and copy to test what your target audience responds to, making sure it's congruent with your landing page and offer.

6. Customize the reports so that you can quickly see what's working and what's not for your predefined campaign goals; that way, you can pause what's not working and scale up and expand what is working.

Chapter 13 Resources:

- Infographic – Downloadable infographic that lays out *The 6 steps of Successful Facebook Ad Campaigns:*

http://www.thebookonfbmarketing.com/resources

Chapter 14

Case Studies – Best Practices and What's Possible with Facebook Ads

-14-

Case Studies – Best Practices and What's Possible with Facebook Ads

Case Study #1: John Lee Dumas of Entrepreneur On Fire – Webinar Funnel FB Ads – Podcaster's Paradise

This first case study goes over the ads I did for John Lee Dumas to get more opt-ins and attendees to his webinars where he was going over the ins and outs of podcasting and selling his Podcasters Paradise program on the back end.

EntrepreneurOnFire.com

Hey, its John Lee Dumas here. 😊 Are you ready to Create ~ Grow ~ & Monetize your Podcast? Join me on my LIVE Podcast Training Workshop where I'll share how you can benefit from the explosive growth of Podcasting and how I personally generate $100,000 a month with my Podcast Entrepreneur On Fire. Click below to claim your spot for the FREE Podcast training!

LIVE Podcast Training Workshop
With John Lee Dumas of Entrepreneur On Fire
Click here and start learning how to create, grow, and monetize your own Podcast.

Sign Up

Like · Comment · Share · 👍 314 💬 27 📄 14 · 👤 · Sponsored (demo)

Notice the personal tone of the post text for the ad? Note how it's written from the WIIFM perspective of the target audience, including what's possible? Notice the smiley face, the use of CAPS, and the tilde to draw additional attention to the post? The last sentence is a call to action. Don't forget your calls to action!

The image is one of John smiling and doing what the ad describes. The headline under the pic reinforces what it's about and with whom it's happening, while once again, the call to action is at the bottom. Remember from the previous chapters that link-share ads with photos that are 1,200 pixels wide x 628 pixels tall work the best.

When I did this ad, the call-to-action buttons had just came out, so they worked very well. I've found them not to work as well since then as people have gotten used to them and associate them with ads. However, that might change once again with the new partner-apps targeting that Facebook just released to all advertisers.

Lastly, the amount of engagement shown with the likes, comments, and shares helps drive the social proof and ends up increasing conversions and reducing lead costs.

EntrepreneurOnFire.com

Hey, John Lee Dumas here. 😊 Are you ready to stab fear in the face and IGNITE your podcast in 2014? Join me on my LIVE Podcast Training Workshop where I'll share how you can benefit from the explosive growth of Podcasting and how I personally generate $100,000 a month with my Podcast Entrepreneur On Fire. Click below to claim your spot for the FREE Podcast training!

LIVE Podcast Training Workshop
With John Lee Dumas of Entrepreneur On Fire
Click here and start learning how to create, grow, and monetize your own Podcast.

Learn More

Like · Comment · Share · 👍 812 💬 81 📝 35 · 🌐 · Sponsored (demo)

This was the second image I used in the newsfeed. The headline and copy remained basically the same. I had tested both the "Sign Up" call-to-action button and the "Learn More" button and found that the "Learn More" button converted the best at the lowest cost.

The key difference was the image. Look at the substantial increase in engagement!

Here's an interesting thing that happened though: While overall, this image got higher conversions at a lower cost, what I found was that women did not care for this image at all and were driving up lead costs. However, men LOVED it! So the solution I came up with was to show image 1 (of John's face) only to women and to show image 2 (of the shark) only to men.

Voila! I maximized lead conversions and lowered costs by aligning the ads with what each group liked the best and with what resonated with them. Testing, my friends, it all comes down to testing and then doing a deep dive into the results!

Both of the examples above were ads I ran in the newsfeed and tested mobile against desktop. As usual, mobile ads converted at a lower opt-in cost, but the desktop ads were the ones that drove the sales on the backside of the webinar.

Here's an example of the ad I ran on the right-hand side the day of the webinar. I LOVE running these right-hand-side ads as reminders for the webinar to those who've already signed up and also as a last-minute nudge for those who haven't signed up yet. Note: this ad ran before the format change on the right-hand-side ads.

Now you're probably wondering what the results were for these ads. Well, my friends, for the first webinar round, twenty out of twenty-six sales came directly from Facebook! To break that down further, ad spend was $1,696, which resulted in $19,940 in sales on the backend of the webinar and which was tied directly to Facebook ads through the conversion tracking pixel (20 sales at $997 per sale).

The other thing that can't be measured is how many people saw that right-hand ad and showed up and purchased because of it? How many people saw the buzz, which sparked them to start following John and Entrepreneur On Fire? Those are the things that are still hard to measure and quantify with Facebook ads, but we know it happens.

Case Study #2: Valerie Shoopman and Nick Unsworth of Life on Fire – Webinar Funnel FB Ads – Facebook Ads A to Z

Nick and I did a Facebook Ads A to Z training course shortly after I ran the ads for John Lee Dumas, and I used the exact same methodology above to make those ads work.

Life on Fire
Sponsored ·

Hey Nick and Valerie here! 😊 Are you ready to learn how to leverage the NEW Facebook Ad changes (New in Feb 2014) to get hundreds of targeted people signed up to your list? PLUS, we'll share our #1 new technique that's literally crushing it right now with a "Celebrity Client" that got him a WHOPPING 1129% ROI on his recent webinar event! Click below to claim your spot for the FREE Facebook Ad training!

Learn How To Leverage FB's Latest Ad Changes

Click here and start learning how to leverage Facebook Ads to build authority and get likes, leads, and new customers with an insane ROI.

WITH NICK UNSWORTH AND VALERIE SHOOPMAN

Unlike · Comment · Share · 👍 158 💬 12 📤 4

Notice the personal voice in the post? Notice the WIIFM perspective of the ideal client? Notice the smiley faces, quotation marks, CAPS, and parentheses that help certain things stand out and grab your attention? And of course, notice the call to action at the end!

Again, the headline and copy below the image make clear what the link is about and what they should do. The engagement on the post encourages others to believe that this is something important and worth their attention.

An interesting thing about this image is that I tested several images with blue, gray, and black for the text and banner, but the pink converted the best with both women and men. The pink pops in the newsfeed and grabs people's attention.

LIVE Facebook Ad Training
lifeonfire.com

Learn how to leverage FB ads to create 5 figures of "net" profit per month!

35,588 people like this

I used the right-hand-side ads in exactly the same way as I did with John Lee Dumas, as a billboard of sorts to stay on the right-hand side of people's Facebook pages all day long on the day of the webinar.

Notice how the pink pops in this ad too. I didn't really mean to "pinkify" Nick, but it was definitely working well, and he said he's really all about the end result. So pink it was!

Speaking of end results ... how about $4,646.96 in ad spend for twenty-five sales of a $997 live training course and a $3,000–per-month elite client? That's $4,646.96

spent to make $60,925. Having the right strategy and the right funnel as well as optimizing our Facebook ads made it all possible.

Case Study #3: Life on Fire Virtual Summit 2014 – Taking the Webinar Funnel to a New Level

What's better than Facebook ads to a webinar funnel? Facebook ads to a Live Virtual Summit where you can showcase others, provide lots of great free content, and bring everyone together to help build a school for children in Guatemala—a win, win, win for everyone involved!

Life on Fire
Sponsored ·

I'm super fired up to bring you this virtual summit with 24 of the most sought after speakers I hand-picked for this special event! They'll be sharing their personal success strategies based around purpose, mindset, marketing, and networking. Our mission is to help you build your business and live a life on fire AND support Pencils of Promise to build a school in Guatemala. Hop on board this puppy to catch the Virtual Success Train and start living a Life On Fire!

FREE Event | Life On Fire Virtual Summit 2014

Click Here To Get Your FREE Access Pass To The Life On Fire Virtual Summit And Start Learning From Today's Top Entrepreneurs!

WITH NICK UNSWORTH AND 24 OF TODAY'S TOP ENTREPRENEURS

Like · Comment · Share · 471 20 74

You can see the ad uses the same setup and structure as those used in the previous case studies. You might be wondering why I keep using this same format. I use it because it flat-out works over and over again in multiple niches with various campaigns. The data proves it in the conversions, lead costs, and ultimately the sales on the backend of the funnels.

You'll notice the same personal copy in the post, along with what we're doing and why we're doing it. The call to action is included, and the headline and copy under the image support the post copy and lets them know what it is, why they'd want to be a part of it, and how to proceed.

While we are still actively running this campaign at the time of this writing, I can tell you that during the initial testing phase we drove 4,277 opt-ins at an average cost per opt-in of $2.57 for very targeted leads. In some cases, I was getting these targeted opt-ins for as low as $0.13 per opt-in. It's crazy to think that's still possible today, right now with Facebook ads!

In this particular Facebook marketing funnel, we did something quite different. Not only did we run ads with the goal of getting opt-ins for the virtual summit, but we also added in a bonus on the thank-you page that was just too sweet to pass up.

WE HAVE A VERY SPECIAL OFFER

WE'RE GIVING IT ALL TO YOU FOR A SMALL DONATION OF ONLY $97

100% of the proceeds go directly towards building a school in Guatemala

FOR A LIMITED TIME, YOU CAN GET THE

BUSINESS ON FIRE BUNDLE

($10,000 value)

The shortcut to massive success and living a Life on Fire is learning from market leaders that have proven strategies that can help you get there faster.

That's exactly why we talked industry leaders into donating their most sought after products & coaching programs into the "Business on Fire Bundle"

Here's what you'll get IF you take action and decide to invest in your success...

The bonus was an offering of several highly valued business products currently selling for a collective price of over $10,000, and we offered it for a mere $97. Plus, the proceeds from the bonus go to Pencils of Promise to build a school for kids in Guatemala.

The key thing was where we put the bonus in the funnel. We put it on the thank-you page that people saw after they opted in for the virtual summit.

Doing it this way allowed us to:

- pay for the Facebook advertising costs as we went
- build a list of targeted buyers willing to get out their credit cards
- sell more bonus packages up front, which will generate more dollars to help Pencils of Promise build the school in Guatemala
- create a win, win, win for everyone involved

Case Study #4: IGNITE Live Event – Direct Sales Funnel

While Facebook ads linked directly to sales pages rarely work, in this case they did with Nick's live event called IGNITE.

A couple reasons why this worked ...

1. While they did have to pay $97, the tickets were actually free because they were going to be refunded that $97 when they arrived at the event.

2.   I ran the ad only to people who were either very closely aligned with Nick and Life on Fire or were within driving distance of San Diego and in the ideal target market.

The end result was an average cost per sale of $35.82 with the lowest cost per sale of $11.57. That's the amount in ad spend to get someone to purchase a ticket to come to the live event where Nick can further the relationship on a very personal level. Not bad, not bad at all!

Life on Fire
Sponsored ·

Hey Nick here and I want to personally invite you to my LIVE December event IGNITE! Oooh it gets even better... I'm hooking you up with a FREE ticket over the next few days!!!

Claim your seat for Ignite for a refundable deposit of just $97 today using the promo code "IGNITE" at http://smarturl.it/IgniteEvent

That's right! Enter the promo code IGNITE to reduce the price to just $97, and when you arrive at the event we'll hand you a check for your $97 right back and you'll ge... See More

3-Day LIVE Mastermind Event | December 5th, 6th, 7th in San Diego, CA

Register today if you have a passion for life AND want to take your business to the next level!

FREE TICKETS FOR A LIMITED TIME!

Unlike · Comment · Share · 👍 194 💬 15 📤 21

You'll notice the same personal tone and WIIFM perspective along with the call to action and engagement.

Notice also how, with just a few words, the copy below the image answers the questions *what, when, where, why,* and *how*. That, my friends, is the secret sauce to this ad!

People want to QUICKLY know what it is, when it is, where it is, why they should go, and how they can attend.

That wraps up the case studies I have for you here, but I did make a video for you in which I go over various other ads and funnels and give you my expert opinion on what makes them winners or losers. You can learn a ton from what others are doing. It's even better with someone guiding you along the way! Check out the ad critique video at

http://www.thebookonfbmarketing.com/resources

I truly hope these case studies along with Nick's strategies and my step-by-step tutorials have given you the knowledge, insight, and creative spark necessary to implement your own Facebook marketing funnels and campaigns that are wildly successful and help propel your business and life to the next level!

I have to say I'm rather sad this book is coming to an end. I LOVE talking about Facebook marketing and how Facebook ads can make such an impact toward building your brand, reaching your ideal clients, generating a targeted e-mail list of buyers and potential buyers, and creating a thriving community of like-minded individuals who willingly share their experiences about your products and services.

Mindset + Strategy + Marketing Funnels + Facebook Ads = A Business and Life on Fire!!

Keep those fires burning brightly and please let us know of your successes and achievements you have utilizing our strategies and methods in *The Book on Facebook Marketing.* We'd love to hear how you are setting your business and life on fire to truly make a difference!

Chapter 14 Recap:

- Link share ads with 1,200 x 628 images work best.
- Use personal, eye-catching photos that convey an emotional response.
- Use a personal voice when creating your ads.
- Make sure you include the WIIFM (What's In It For Me) perspective of your ideal client.
- If possible, quickly tell them the *what, when, where, why,* and *how* about your offer.
- Always include a call to action.
- Test to see if what you think will work actually does. The clicks will define the clear winner, not your ego.

Chapter 14 Resources:

- Podcaster's Paradise –
  http://smarturl.it/PodcastWebinar
- Facebook Ads A to Z course –
  http://lifeonfire.com/facebook
- Virtual Summit page –
  http://lifeonfirevirtualsummit.com
- Business On Fire Bundle –
  http://businessonfirebundle.com
- Ignite – http://igniteevent2014.com
- Life on Fire website – http://lifeonfire.com
- Video – *Facebook Ad Critique*

http://www.thebookonfbmarketing.com/resources

ABOUT NICK UNSWORTH

I was six years old when I picked up my first pack of matches.

Wait. That makes me sound like a pyro. What I mean is that my own entrepreneurial fire started at a very young age.

You see, my mother emboldened me with the idea that I could do anything and be anything if I put my mind to it. I proved her right at a young age by running a paper route empire at age 6 (maybe not an empire, but still, I was a balling 6-year old).

Growing up, I watched my friends' parents struggle with money. I saw the toll it took on their families and remember vividly them not being able to attend the important things like little league games because they were always working. I remember stories of uncertainty that comes from working for other people.

I vowed to never let that be me.

I've been an entrepreneur on a mission for about 11 years now. Here's my journey…

MY FIRST HOME RUN

While in college I discovered network marketing and built a very successful business. I made the typical mistakes of a reckless 21 year old...I leased a $50k car and was spending money recklessly. Sure enough the parent company that I was selling products for went belly up out of the blue.

That's when I experienced my first true hardship. I literally lost it all and then found myself 30k in debt going from business opportunity to business opportunity.

CHASING THE DREAM INTO THE REAL ESTATE INDUSTRY

I then got things together and jumped into the real estate business. This was is 2005 mind you. I missed the whole bubble where money was raining out of the sky but I figured I could build a good lifestyle from it.

In 2007 I ended up moving to San Diego to work on a lending project for the Hard Rock Hotel. Not more than 2 weeks after I landed the US economy experiences the "mortgage meltdown" which was the biggest financial catastrophe since the great depression. Again, I found myself up shit's creek and was left in a tough spot.

In 2008 I returned home to CT where I focused on building my real estate business and knew that I needed to get my name out in the marketplace as fast as possible.

CREATING MY FIRST BUSINESS THAT GIVES BACK

That's when my new venture the "NU Perks Card" was born. It was a not-for-profit business where I got 45 local businesses in town to put discounts on my NU Perks Card. It looked like a business card that folded out that was meant to carry in your wallet or purse. Basically, consumers could go to some of the nicest restaurants in town and flash their NU Perks Card and get 15% off the bill or half off a bottle of wine etc.

I built NU Perks Card.com to sell them for $20 each. From there, $10 of the purchase went to the charity of their choice. My goal was to get my name out in the community while raising thousands for non-profits. When I launched the business I made a huge mistake. I went against my gut and trusted a "traditional" advertising company that recommended TV commercials.

All said and done I spent about 50k launching the business and things were rocking. I was featured on "Better Connecticut" which is a morning show, I was all over the papers in town and things couldn't be better. The problem was that the advertising was insanely expensive and the ROI was unbelievably negative. I pulled the plug on the costly TV commercials and I experienced something that would change my life forever...my website was ranked on the first page of Google.

Even after I pulled down my marketing the traffic kept coming and coming. It was unbelievable to experience the power of Google. Furthermore, a large national company that had a similar name saw that I was ranked higher than them on Google and decided to sue me for Trademark infringement. Long story short I didn't have the capital to fight it so I had to take the business down.

LOSING IT ALL

So again I found myself on the verge of bankruptcy trying to figure out the next business that I was going to start. Quitting and getting a job definitely crossed my mind as I was living off of credit cards but I kept clinging to the hope of actually finding my passion and loving what I do.

That's when I got into internet marketing. I spent a good year and half learning everything from everyone. I was traveling the country on credit cards going from conference to conference to figure out how I could build an online business. I was so broke that I would bring protein powder with me in sandwich bags and sneak up to my hotel room when everyone else was enjoying meals together.

I was at the proverbial rock bottom but knew that the pain was temporary. I saw an opportunity with Facebook marketing and I decided to dive right in and take no prisoners.

GETTING MY MOJO BACK

I built out my blog www.nickunsworth.com, my fan page and officially stopped selling houses for my real estate business. At that point, I was in severe debt and had to figure out how to pay my bills that were just over $3,500 per mo because my credit card debt was close to $1,200 per mo.

I made the leap of faith, started NU Media 2.0 and picked up my first 5 clients within 30 days and was able to pay my bills. From there, I worked my tail off and started helping clients get results online and it started to snowball. By my 90th day I had trained over 50 businesses and was starting to pick up speaking engagements.

By my 4th month I landed a $50,000 contract for 90 days and then things just exploded. I ended up picking up larger clients like Keller Williams Realty, BMW, and others. This has led to a complete transformation in my life and in business.

I quickly paid off my debt and was rocking and rolling. I continued to train over 1,100 business owners and entrepreneurs how to get customers using Facebook marketing. Along the way I built a Facebook application called "**Fan Reviews**."

SELLING A BUSINESS BY THE AGE OF 30

The tool created incredible results for my clients and as a result I had multiple offers to buy equity into my business. Selling a business had been my dream for years and I even have a tattoo on my chest of the goal. How's that for goal setting!? It worked.

Since that experience I went on to sell the rest of my shares in the business so that I could put 100% of my focus on helping entrepreneurs build kick ass lives and businesses that have real purpose and meaning.

AND THAT'S WHEN LIFE ON FIRE WAS BORN!

It's truly amazing what happens when you're in "alignment" with what your "purpose" is in life. I now know that my purpose is helping other people and love every minute of every day making Life on Fire a "journey worth living."

My hope is that my story makes you stop and think about your life and your business. Are you doing what you love?

You can do anything you put your mind to and I hope that you are pursuing you're your dreams. Life is too short not to.

Either way, if you made it this far I'd love to hear your thoughts and feedback. Also, if you've found your passion and you're living out your dreams then share your story with me via the comments below.

Looking forward to speaking soon,

Nick

ABOUT VALERIE SHOOPMAN

I have always been a quick learner and loved to be on the leading edge of things, especially things others found difficult. I've had a gift from a very young age to be able to break down and explain complex things in a simple, easy-to-understand format.

When I was a Sophomore in high school, I took an aptitude test and scored extremely high in the electrical and mechanical section along with the visualization section. Yep, visualization, you know where a 3d diagram is folded multiple ways, but flat on paper and you have to figure out what it looks like from unfolded to folded or vice versa. I love doing that in my mind to this day!

So since I scored high in the electrical section and there was a Vo-Tech associated with my high school that had a great electronics program with an old Navy guy as the teacher, I signed up and loved it. The material just came to me naturally it seemed. I went on from there to go to DeVry and get a degree in electronics. I was one of the three women in a class of 700. Approximately one-half of the class made it to graduation (it was a very accelerated course) and only one female. That female was me and I went on to work in a male-dominated surveying field as an electronics technician and then on to technical support where I provided phone support and training on GPS, GIS and Roading software.

I've long had a love of teaching and that continuously wants to come out in whatever I do! I developed a national training facility for that surveying company and then eventually went on to work at a small private school for kids with learning disabilities training both the staff and students on how to best utilize technology. I built up the technology infrastructure at the school including 3 servers, 6 desktops in each classroom, laptops for the teachers, a rolling iBook computer lab, and researched and implemented different learning/teaching software applications that students and staff could utilize to expand their knowledge and facilitate their growth. I also set up the school's website, optimized it for SEO, and was actively involved in marketing the school to potential students and their parents.

During this time period, I was an affiliate marketer at night and on the weekends and used Google Adwords to drive traffic to the various affiliate offers. Since I was one of the early adopters of Google Adwords, I knew right away when they came out with their Google grants program and secured that for the school. This allowed me to further my knowledge and refine my methods using Google Adwords to drive traffic.

Then along came social media and I jumped on that bandwagon too! I started using Facebook, Twitter, and LinkedIn with Facebook being my favorite. I took a few online courses and attended a few events then started doing all of the school's social media. Before long, lots of friends were coming to me asking me to help them set up their Facebook business pages.

Eventually, I decided I could help more people via social media so I began doing that full-time. About a year after I made that transition, I met Nick Unsworth. He taught me a few things I didn't know about marketing and then I turned around and taught him a few things too about Facebook ads and how to get real results. Long story short, Nick ended up hiring me to do Life On Fire's Facebook ads and social media content. We went on to do several courses on Facebook ads together and the rest, as they say, is history!

I'm looking forward to hearing your comments about "The Book On Facebook Marketing" and helping you stay on the leading edge of what's working in the digital marketing world.

Wishing you much success,

Valerie

CONNECT WITH NICK

Facebook:

https://www.facebook.com/nickunsworthlifeonfire

Twitter:

https://twitter.com/nickunsworth

YouTube:

https://www.youtube.com/user/LifeOnFireTV

CONNECT WITH VAL

Facebook:

http://ValsFanPage.com

Twitter:

https://twitter.com/valshoopman

YouTube:

https://www.youtube.com/user/ValerieShoopman

Linked In:

www.linkedin.com/in/valerieshoopman

IN GRATITUDE TO YOU....

Thank you for your generosity in purchasing *The Book on Facebook Marketing*. Proceeds from the sales of this book will benefit **Pencils of Promise,** a non-profit organization that builds schools and increases educational opportunities in the developing world.

We would be so grateful if you could take a minute or two to share what you loved about this book and provide an honest review on our Amazon sales page.

Made in the USA
San Bernardino, CA
11 May 2016